ESPN

THE
MIGHTY
BOOK OF
SPORTS
KNOWLEDGE

ESPN

THE

MIGHTY

BOOK OF

SPORTS

KNOWLEDGE

EDITED BY

Steve Wulf

BALLANTINE BOOKS · NEW YORK

ESPN
BOOKS

Published in the United States by ESPN Books, an imprint of ESPN, Inc., New York, and Ballantine Books,
an imprint of The Random House Publishing Group, a division of Random House, Inc., New York.

BALLANTINE and colophon are registered trademarks of Random House, Inc.
The ESPN Books name and logo are registered trademarks of ESPN, Inc.

Permission credits can be found on page 209.

ISBN 978-0-345-51177-5

Printed in the United States of America on acid-free paper

www.ballantinebooks.com
www.espnbooks.com

9 8 7 6 5 4 3 2 1

First Edition

Design: BTDnyc

Contents

*Native American
youths in Florida
circa 1564 shoot
arrows, throw balls
at targets placed
atop poles, and run
races. This
engraving, inspired
by the paintings of
sixteenth-century
explorer Jacques le
Moyne de Morgues,
was originally
published in 1591.*

Introduction

BY STEVE WULF

A Babe Parilli leather helmet. A program autographed by Babe Ruth. A Mickey Mantle Louisville Slugger bat. A bowling pin signed by members of the PBA tour. A Jerry West figurine. An empty bag of 4 Bagger chewing tobacco. A Bo Belinsky button. A Bo Jackson Raiders jersey.

Those are just some of the things I've acquired over time. A lot of stuff, most of it scattered about my office, much of it having to do with baseball: a Carl Yastrzemski McDonald's glass, an ancient catcher's mask, two seats from Memorial Stadium in Baltimore, a Russian baseball poster, a sanitary sock once worn by Doc Gooden, a ball autographed by the members of the 1936 Washington Senators, an old portable typewriter, a lineup card from the 1993 World Series, a T-shirt that reads I COVERED THE PINE TAR GAME. And a lot of years, most of them spent as a sportswriter who's often on the lookout for something that evokes the past or celebrates the moment.

My secret vice is pulling over at antiques stores or flea markets. I once tried to buy a Duke Snider bat at an antiques store in Westmoreland, New York, only to be told it was not for sale. "That's what I use to confront shoplifters," said the lady proprietor. No bat, but I did get a San Francisco Giants calendar with all three Alou brothers (Felipe, Matty, and Jesus) on the cover.

In its own way, this book is kind of a flea market. A lot of stuff. A lot of years. There are anecdotes, arguments, quotes, quizzes, lists, lessons, histories, mysteries, speeches, facts, curios. It's haphazard enough that you can drop in anywhere. But it also has a logic to it that will become apparent as you leaf through the pages.

I should point out that I am not the sole proprietor of the book. Most of these items were suggested or written by others: colleagues at *ESPN The Magazine*, ESPN Books, and Ballantine; friends and family; fellow youth coaches; profes-

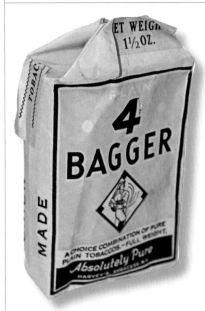

An empty bag of 4 Bagger tobacco.

sional acquaintances. What they all had in common was a curiosity about sports: these are some of the things they wanted to know more about. There are 101 entries here, as well as an almost equal number of random oddities and quotes.

As for the title, the "Mighty" is meant to be both playful and folksy. You may have noticed a spate of sports books out there that assert to be about "The Greatest" game, or "The Last" season, or "The One True" athlete. We make no claim that this is an omnipotent, all-encompassing book. The sports world is so huge, so old, so fascinating, that no one book could pretend to be definitive. We just think this book is mighty interesting.

Within its pages are a lot of things you may not already have in your grasp. Ways to jump rope like Sugar Shane Mosley, or run pass patterns like Jerry Rice, or tape a hockey stick like Wayne Gretzky. Food for arguments about the best sports books, the worst sports movies, the greatest athlete to wear the number 32. Stories about the woman most responsible for Title IX, the fight that broke out among Santa Clauses, the clubhouse attendant who scored a touchdown. Tours of Donovan McNabb's locker, the Seven Wonders of the Sports World, Phil Mickelson's golf bag. The truth about the Gipper, the chances of becoming a pro, the reason why the Tour de France leader wears yellow. And while you're browsing, you'll encounter Yogi Berra, Chris Paul, Carol Channing, Wilt

A Russian baseball poster.

Chamberlain, Bobby Jones, Cal Ripken, Jim Valvano, John Wooden, Gertrude Ederle, Michael Phelps, Babe Ruth, Lou Gehrig . . .

Among my most prized possessions is the wooden frame that once housed Carl Hubbell's original Hall of Fame plaque. Back in the late '70s, before memorabilia became a business, the Baseball Hall of Fame revamped its gallery and simply discarded the frames. Some of them ended up with the proprietor of the batting cage adjacent to Doubleday Field, who sold them for modest prices based on the inhabitant's fame. (If I recall correctly, Candy Cummings went for $12.)

The plaque has been replaced by a mirror, not for the sake of vanity, but for the purpose of reflection. Think of Hubbell, then think of all the athletes who came before and after him. Think of the time Ty Cobb cut Hubbell from the Detroit Tigers, then think of all the similar surprises offered by sports. Think of that screwball of his, then think about all the tricks of the trades. Think of the 1934 All-Star Game in which Hubbell struck out, in succession, Babe Ruth, Lou Gehrig, Jimmie Foxx, Al Simmons, and Joe Cronin, then think about all the great athletic feats.

That's what we call mighty.

—STEVE WULF

FOLLOWING SPREAD:

The Great International Caledonian Games, Jones Woods, New York City, July 1, 1867.

SOCK IT AWAY
JOHN WOODEN ON THE IMPORTANCE OF HOSIERY

It starts with the socks. That's what longtime (1948–75) UCLA basketball coach John Wooden believed, so that was the first thing he taught his incoming Bruins. As one of his players, Bill Walton, recalls, "Here we are, these eager young men ready to learn the key that will unlock it all from the greatest college basketball mind the world has ever known, and he says, 'I'm going to show you how to put on your socks.' And now we're saying to ourselves, 'I'm a high school All-America. Who is this antique?'"

According to Wooden, "I personally demonstrated how I wanted the players to put on their socks: Carefully roll the socks down over the toes, paying special attention to having the seam going horizontally over the toes. Then proceed with bringing the sock over the ball of the foot, arch, and around the heel; then pull the sock up snug so there will be no wrinkles of any kind."

Actually, there were two pairs of socks. The coach wanted the first pair turned inside out so that the softer part would be against the skin. The outer sock would go on normally over the first sock. "I would then have the players carefully check with their fingers for any folds or creases in the sock. I paid special attention to the heel because this is where the wrinkles are most likely. . . . This may seem like a nuisance, trivial, but I had a very practical reason for being meticulous about this. Wrinkles, folds, and creases can cause blisters. Blisters interfere with performance during practice and games."

As for shoes, Wooden wanted them to fit snugly, with very little room at the toe, and he wanted them tied tightly—"start at the bottom of the laces, snug, snug, snug"—with a double knot.

"We came to realize," says Walton, "that the simple process of putting on your socks the right way led to everything else. He never told us the answers, just how to get there. To this day, though, I can't lose the image of him, barefoot in the locker room. Coach Wooden, I'm afraid, had very ugly feet."

> **"There are certain things you can't get back, like the elastic in your socks."**
> —trainer Eddie Futch on boxing comebacks

Coach Wooden talks with Lew Alcindor (Kareem Abdul-Jabbar) and other UCLA freshmen, 1965.

UNTOUCHABLE JERRY RICE ON HOW TO RUN A PASS PATTERN

What if you were going out for a pass in touch football and had the benefit of the experience, if not the talent, of someone who had caught 1,549 passes for 22,895 yards and 197 touchdowns in the NFL? What route would you run?

Meet Jerry Rice.

First of all, touch football is fantastic. It's all about quickness and being elusive. You can really focus on your routes and on catching the ball without worrying about getting killed.

The number one thing is, don't let them get their hands on you. If you can get off the line cleanly, there's nothing they can do to stop you. I'd run a post route in the middle of the field, then, once I got to the red zone, put a double move on and run a post corner. That's like taking candy from a baby.

Pick routes are also great. If you can have your second WR come across the middle and reroute that linebacker a little bit, the number one guy will be wide open in the flat. It's just up to the QB to get him the ball.

Rice says that just as in pro football, the QB and his receivers have to be on the same page in touch football.

If your QB is having a bad day, run a couple of safer routes and build his confidence back up. Then you can go for the home run ball. And stay positive. Bill Walsh used to tell us, 'If you don't feel like you have a chance of winning, then you're already defeated.' That's just as true in touch as it is in tackle."

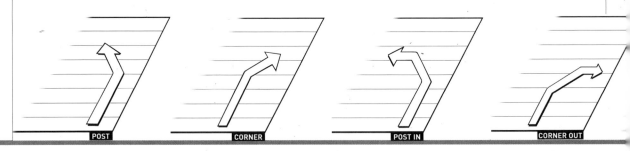

POST   CORNER   POST IN   CORNER OUT

CLEAR

John Heisman, for whom the award is named, coached Georgia Tech to a 222–0 win over Cumberland College in 1916. He had his reasons: 1) he wanted to avenge a 22–0 loss to Cumberland in baseball earlier in the year and 2) he wanted to show sportswriters that point totals should not be factored into the voting for national champions.

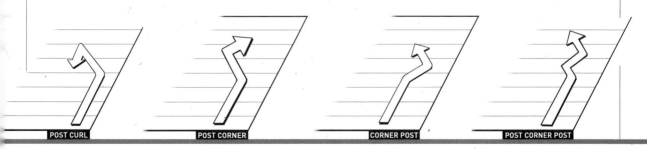

POST CURL   POST CORNER   CORNER POST   POST CORNER POST

THE PITS 13 SECONDS WITH A NASCAR PIT CREW

They don't sell Caleb Hurd T-shirts at Walmart, but they should. The former Virginia Tech holder on placekicks now handles the gas can for Jeff Gordon's Rainbow Warriors, NASCAR's most storied pit crew. Says Hurd, "Jeff can drive his guts out for 40 laps, and then we can undo everything with one bad stop. It makes handling a kick in the BCS title game feel like a walk in the park."

What's the big deal? Let's take a look inside a four-tire, two-cans-of-fuel Sprint Cup pit stop—13 seconds of beautifully brutal ballet:

1. The driver brings his 3,400-pound race car to a perfect stop inside the white-lined pit box, allowing enough room between his left side and the wall for the crew to work, but not stopping so far right that they're in harm's way. Seven men go over the wall while another half dozen provide support behind it.

2. The jack man slings his 45-pound aluminum jack around to the passenger side, and after him come two tire changers and two tire carriers toting a pair of 75-pound tires. With one stroke, the car rises as the tire changers pop off five lug nuts with their air wrenches.

3. The gas man is already emptying the first of two 11-gallon, 70-pound cans of fuel, which are guided into the nozzle by his assistant, the catch-can man. When the first is empty, he tosses it over the wall and is handed the second.

4. As the changers pull off the old right-side rubber, the carriers slap two new ones onto the studs. Five fresh lugs are preglued to the wheel wells, firmly enough to stick but loosely enough to let the wrenches do the job. The carriers and the jack man chase down the old tires, which will incur a NASCAR penalty if they roll out of the pit box.

5. The instant the last lug is tight, the jack drops, and everyone heads over to the other side, careful not to trip over the air hoses, slip on the white pit-box paint, or crash into the fuelers at the rear of the car.

> **Jeff Gordon's first NASCAR race, in November of 1992, was Richard Petty's last.**

6. The process is then repeated on the left side of the ride.
7. Once the old tires are behind the wall, the tire carriers busy themselves scraping trash off the front grille, cleaning the windshield by pulling away a Mylar tear-off, or making a chassis adjustment by snapping a ratchet wrench into the back windshield to raise or lower the rear of the car.

Gordon's pit crew races the clock on June 8, 2008, during the NASCAR Sprint Cup Series Pocono 500 at Pocono International Raceway in Long Pond, Pennsylvania.

8. Everyone waits on the fuel man to finish filling, which is signified when gas starts to overflow into the catch-can man's . . . well, you guessed it—into his catch can.
9. With a twist of the handle, the jack man drops the car to the ground, which is the driver's signal to drop the hammer—but not too hard. If he exceeds the 55 mph pit-road speed limit, he's coming back around for a stop-and-go penalty.
10. If all of the above happens in 13 seconds or less, congratulations! You're still in the race.

LARCENOUS LOU

SITTING DOWN? LOU GEHRIG STOLE HOME 15 TIMES

The numbers that Lou Gehrig is usually associated with are 4 (his uniform), 23 (the record for career grand slams), and 2,130 (the record for consecutive games played, until Cal Ripken broke it). But there is one number belonging to Larrupin' Lou that might surprise you: 15. That's how many times Gehrig stole home in his career.

Although that's nowhere near the record of 54 set by Ty Cobb, it is 15 more than the total of Lou Brock, who had 938 steals in his career, 836 more than Gehrig had in his. As you may have already guessed, stealing home was a more popular ploy when Gehrig was playing than it is nowadays. In fact, the only post–

New York Yankee Lou Gehrig slides into home plate past Washington catcher Hank Severeid, 1925.

World War II players with more steals of home than Gehrig are Jackie Robinson (19) and Rod Carew (17).

Though the Iron Horse carried the alternative sobriquets Piano Legs and Biscuit Pants, he did have decent speed. All of his home thefts came on the front end of double steals, when he was on third and another runner was on first—if the opposing catcher threw down to second, Gehrig broke for home. (The tactic lives on in Little League.) The first of those steals of home was actually and anomalously Gehrig's first career stolen base.

Because they were known as Murderers' Row, the Yankees seldom got credit for their aggressive baserunning. But twice Babe Ruth stole second as Gehrig broke from third, the first time in the 1st inning, the second time in the 3rd. Thanks to Raymond J. Gonzalez of *The Baseball Research Journal,* here is a complete list of Gehrig's home invasions:

6/24/25 vs. Washington: double steal in 7th with Wally Schang

4/13/26 vs. Boston: double steal in 1st with Babe Ruth

7/24/26 vs. Chicago: double steal in 3rd with Babe Ruth

6/11/27 vs. Cleveland: double steal in 5th with Tony Lazzeri

6/29/27 vs. Boston: double steal in 8th with Bob Meusel

7/30/27 vs. Cleveland (first game): double steal in 3rd with Bob Meusel

7/19/29 vs. Cleveland (first game): double steal in 2nd with Cedric Durst

6/7/30 vs. St. Louis: double steal in 6th with Bill Dickey

4/15/31 vs. Boston: double steal in 8th with Tony Lazzeri

7/28/31 vs. Chicago: double steal in 5th with Ben Chapman

4/12/32 vs. Philadelphia: double steal in 9th with Ben Chapman

6/20/33 vs. Chicago: double steal in 6th with Tony Lazzeri

6/28/33 vs. Detroit: double steal in 9th with Ben Chapman

6/2/34 vs. Philadelphia: double steal in 1st with Jack Saltzgaver

5/15/35 vs. Detroit: double steal in 7th with Tony Lazzeri

If you still doubt Lou Gehrig had speed, consider this: He also had six inside-the-park home runs.

WHISTLE WHILE YOU WORK
HOW TO WHISTLE LIKE A MAJOR LEAGUER

Wanna be a major league baseball coach? Here's a little tip that may help you land that job some day: Nearly every team in baseball has a designated whistler, somebody who can get the attention of an out-of-position outfielder or alert an infielder to a bunt by putting two fingers in his mouth and letting loose an end-of-shift-quality whistle. And even if you don't get the job, these tips will help you hail cabs or herd cattle or harass the other contestants:

Step 1. Wash your hands!

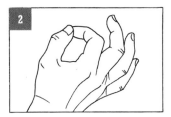  

Step 2. Use your index finger and thumb to form an oval, as you would to form the OK sign.

Step 3. Curl your tongue up and place the tips of your fingers (your thumb and index finger), still forming an oval, under the tip of your tongue.

Step 4. Insert the fingers into your mouth up to about the first knuckle. Place them on the center of your bottom lip, which should be taut. Then, wrap your upper lip over your fingers and tongue. Depending on the size of your mouth, you may be able to wrap your lips over your teeth as well and then press your fingers against your tongue.

Step 5. Here comes the tricky part. The angle of your tongue, teeth, and fingers form what's called a bevel, and the sound of the whistle is the result of air flowing over that bevel. You are essentially creating a blowhole, and you want to channel the air through it to achieve a crisp whistle. Apply pressure to your fingers with your tongue, keep air from creeping out of the corners of your mouth, and blow.

Everyone's whistling apparatus is different, so you will have to adjust lip placement, finger angles, blowhole size, tongue pressure, and moisture in the mouth until you find a system that works for you. Make small changes, and you will gradually go from hearing a gush of air to hearing the kind of piercing whistle that would get Manny Ramirez to move to his left.

Until you master it, though, you might want to get a bib.

> The team doctor for the 1908 New York Giants, Joseph Creamer, was banned from baseball for trying to bribe an umpire $2,500 to help the Giants beat the Cubs.

"Why should I be old-fashioned just because I'm old?"
—Casey Stengel

SPECIAL K

WHY *K* STANDS FOR STRIKEOUT

Maybe you know how to work a box score. Maybe you love to paste up a long row of *K*s when your team's pitcher blows away the other guys. You may even think it's cool that Roger Clemens named his sons Kory, Koby, Kacy, and Kody. But do you know why we use the letter *K*—not the letter *S*—to stand for "strikeout"?

The credit for this quirky bit of sports notation goes to Henry Chadwick, who was born in England and moved with his family to Brooklyn at the age of 12. There, he played cricket and other early ball games, such as rounders. Eventually, Chadwick went to work as a sportswriter for various New York papers, mostly covering cricket matches. He reportedly first encountered baseball in 1856 and almost immediately got hooked on the game. He soon abandoned the wickets in favor of the diamond. Along the way, he developed the box score, the basic template of which has changed only slightly since its inception, and the notations used with it. (He was also the first to calculate such statistical measures as ERA and batting average.)

Henry Chadwick, circa 1890.

Chadwick, whose contributions to the game earned him induction into the Hall of Fame in Cooperstown, apparently favored the last letters of words as much as the first. He explained his method in such volumes as the *Beadle's Dime Base-Ball Player of 1861,* among the first books to catalog the rules of the game and from which the following is excerpted:

In order, also, to record the movements of each player during the game, a series of abbreviations are adopted, those we use in scoring being as follows:

A for first base.	D for catch on the bound.
B for second base.	L for foul balls.
C for third base.	T for tips.
H for home base.	K for struck out.
F for catch on the fly.	R for run out between bases.

Double letters—

H R, or h r, for home runs.

L F for foul ball on the fly.

L D for foul ball on the bound.

T F for tip on the fly.

T D for tip on the bound.

The above, at first sight, would appear to be a complicated alphabet to remember, but when the key is applied, it will be at once seen that a boy could easily impress it on his memory in a few minutes. The explanation is simply this—we use the first letter in the words Home, Fly, and Tip, and the last in Bound, Foul, and Struck, and the first three letters of the alphabet for the first three bases.

Got it? We actually prefer the simplicity of one of Phil Rizzuto's scorecard notations: WW. That stood for "Wasn't Watching."

Beadle's Dime Base-ball Player *of 1873.*

IN THE BAG

You know what's in your golf bag: eight used golf balls, a crumpled scorecard, and a golf glove that you've been wearing since your last birdie, six months ago. But do you know what's in Phil Mickelson's golf bag? Here to tell you is Jim "Bones" Mackay, Lefty's longtime caddy:

We travel with 16 or 17 clubs, so each week we have to figure out what's in and what's out, depending on the course and weather conditions. We haven't played many tournaments this year with a 3-iron, but we did last week in Atlanta because of the long par 3s. Phil won Colonial with five wedges, and there were a few other tournaments where we had that setup.

He shows up at the beginning of the week with every-thing, and it's my job to make sure we've got in there what we need. He'll have rain pants, a short-sleeve rain top and a long-sleeve rain top, of course the umbrella, and the cover for the top of the bag should it start raining. I check the weather every evening before we go out.

When you get into the pockets, there's a ton of things in there. Obviously, you've got the tees and the balls, 12 every day for us. We almost always use be-tween six and nine balls.

We've never come close to running out until last week in Atlanta, when we started to talk about having to use used balls. He made five birdies in seven holes and started handing them out to kids. I probably should have been quicker to warn him about that. He played the last three holes with the same ball. It was kind of oval at the end, but he was making birdies, so it didn't matter.

If I have time, I'll mark them all before the round, but usually there's so much going on, watching the warm-up, getting pin sheets, rules sheets, wiping down grips. . . . Sometimes you don't have quite enough time to mark 12 balls. It takes a little more time than you might think.

Food's a necessity. I buy and pack two different kinds of energy bars that he likes. Sometimes there are snacks out there, but you can't count on them. When we play in the last group on the last day, there's a couple of crumbs left. There's water on the tees, but we always carry it in the bag because you can go through it quickly. Depending on the weather, he can drink seven, eight, nine bottles of water, if not more.

Let's see, two or three training aids that he uses for his putting drills. There's Advil, allergy medicine, an extra pair of contacts, contact solution, sunscreen. Sharpies. Very critical, Sharpies, (a) for marking balls, (b) for autographs afterward. Pencils. There's a rule sheet for each particular week. Lead tape, laser, the shaft Phil uses to check his alignment on the range. Adhesive tape if his hand cracks a little bit when he's practicing hard. Gloves, four, five, six, something like that. He's not a long-tee guy. He likes white golf tees, not the old-timey short white ones, but—I don't know—$2\frac{1}{4}$ inches? They're very hard to find on the road, so I've got to bring them.

I'm not real sure what the bag weighs. Callaway makes a heckuva golf bag. It's not so much the dead weight as much as how well the weight is distributed, and the Callaway bags are fantastic in that sense. They're not particularly heavy. I'm totally guessing here, 45 pounds or so loaded.

More if we're playing at Pebble Beach, though. There, I carry everything that we've named, plus a sweater, a sweater vest, and mittens.

> "The more I practice, the luckier I get."
> —former PGA golfer Jerry Barber

GENIUS IN A JIFFY
THE FIVE BEST SPORTS LEADS

The creed of the sportswriter is Write better than anybody faster than you and faster than anybody better than you. With that in mind, we present five examples of timeless leads written while the clock was ticking:

Reporters at New York's Polo Grounds during the 1913 World Series.

"Outlined against a blue-gray October sky, the Four Horsemen rode again. In dramatic lore they are known as Famine, Pestilence, Destruction and Death. These are only aliases. Their real names are: Stuhldreher, Miller, Crowley and Layden."

—Grantland Rice, *New York Herald Tribune,* on Notre Dame's 13–7 victory over Army on October 13, 1924

"Now it is done. Now the story ends. And there is no way to tell it. The art of fiction is dead. Reality has strangled invention. Only the utterly impossible, the inexpressibly fantastic, can ever be plausible again."

—Red Smith, *New York Herald Tribune,* on Bobby Thomson's home run off Ralph Branca, which gave the New York Giants a 5–4 victory over the Brooklyn Dodgers in their final playoff game in 1951

"Olympic Village was under siege. Two men lay murdered and eight others were held at gunpoint in imminent peril of their lives. Still the games went on. Canoeists paddled through their races. Fencers thrust and parried in make-believe duels. Boxers scuffled. Basketball players scampered across the floor like happy children. Walled off in their dream world, appallingly unaware of the realities of life and death, the aging playground directors who conduct this quadrennial muscle dance ruled that a little bloodshed must not be permitted to interrupt play."

—Red Smith, *The New York Times,* at the 1972 Munich Olympics

"For those of you who missed the Russo-Finnish War, the Johnstown Flood and Custer's Last Stand, be of good cheer. Muhammad Ali is going to 'fight' Chuck Wepner, Type O. Like the *Titanic* fought that iceberg."

—Jim Murray, *Los Angeles Times,* previewing the 1975 Wepner-Ali fight

"They played like it was the seventh game of the World Series."

—Peter Pascarelli, *The Baltimore News-American,* after the Pittsburgh Pirates beat the Baltimore Orioles in the seventh game of the 1979 World Series

You may have noticed that Red Smith wrote two of those. Yes, he was that good and that fast.

THE WRITE STUFF DAVID WRIGHT ON HOW TO GET AN AUTOGRAPH

Back in 1995, Jason Isringhausen was a 22-year-old pitcher for the Norfolk Tides, then the Mets' triple-A affiliate. Somewhere in the crowd of kids always asking for his autograph at Harbor Park was a 12-year-old named David Wright. Years later, they would meet again, Isringhausen as the closer for the St. Louis Cardinals and Wright as the third baseman for the Mets.

Having been on both sides of the pen, Wright has a special appreciation for the right way to ask for an autograph: "I would say 'please' and 'thank you,' and that's what I listen for as a player. It sounds simple, but as players we really appreciate politeness because people look at us differently sometimes and take things for granted."

Here are some basic rules to follow if you're looking for autographs:

1. **Be polite.** Try saying "Mr. Brady" instead of shouting "Hey, Tom!" Players are attuned to the people in a crowd, and they'll often overlook the pushy autograph seekers and seek out kids who are being shoved aside. Nice guys do finish first.

2. **Be patient.** It's a little like fishing: Get to an event early, scope out the best locations, and wait. "During batting practice," says Wright, "find the path a player takes from the field to the dugout. Try to catch his attention, but don't be overbearing." A less crowded spot in which to wait is along the outfield lines, where players usually do their stretching. There are also opportunities after a game, but you have to be *very* patient for those.

3. **Be prepared.** Bring along a pen, preferably a Sharpie, which now comes in a miniature version. Bring along something to sign: a ball, a hat, a card, a program. "Doesn't matter what," says Wright. Keep a roster or lineup handy to help identify players and coaches.

4. **Be organized.** What you do with the autograph after an event is just as important as what you do to get it. If thrown cavalierly into a sock drawer after the game, it is liable to sit around so long it becomes unrecognizable. So keep a special place for the signatures, out of the direct sunlight.

1 8   THE WRITE STUFF

5. Don't be particular.

While everyone clamors for the big stars to sign, other players go unnoticed. You never know what will become of them. Brett Favre was once a third-string quarterback, Albert Pujols an unknown rookie. Minor league ballparks are especially good places for autographs: not as much competition, and in a year or two that signature may be attached to a much bigger name.

By the way, Wright may have Isringhausen's name, but Isringhausen has Wright's number: 0-for-6 lifetime.

> **The number of baseballs used during a major league game is between five dozen and six dozen (60–72).**

THROWDOWN THE SECRETS TO ROCK, PAPER, SCISSORS

In Korea, it's known as *gawi, bawi, bo.* In Germany, it's *Schnik, Schnak, Schnuk.* In Chile, *ca, chi, pun.* You know it as rock, paper, scissors, and it's a game as universal and ancient as football. At the same time as your opponent, you throw out your hand in the symbol of one of three objects: rock takes scissors, scissors take paper, paper takes rock. Could be one and done or best of three or a World Series–like best of seven. But you know all that. And you probably think it's pretty much a matter of luck.

Wrong, says Graham Walker, a co-founder of the World RPS Society. "It is not a game of random chance because both players have to make a choice about what throw to pick. There's always something motivating our actions." Walker's advice boils down to play paper, play quickly, and play opposites. As he explains, "Rock is for rookies, the most common throw for beginners, so play paper instead. The less time you let your opponent think between throws, the more likely they will be to fall into a predictable pattern. Finally, players have a tendency—when rushed—to play the throw that you last played."

For more advanced players, there are gambits, like "the avalanche," three successive rocks. There's also "cloaking," which is waiting until the last nanosecond to reveal your throw, and "player profiling," in which you study your opponents' tells and dominant throws.

So, no, it's not all luck. Not even if you're playing *kamen, papir, makaze* in Bosnia.

REEL GOOD
JEFFREY LYONS PICKS THE FIVE BEST SPORTS MOVIES

Since the inception of the **Academy Awards in 1929,** 13 sports movies have been nominated for Best Picture (or the equivalent award). But which movies have been the best sports pictures? We asked the noted film critic and sports expert Jeffrey Lyons for his five best, and oddly enough none of them has ever been nominated for Best Picture. Here are his choices, with a trailer from each:

Field of Dreams **(1989, baseball).**

"It was like coming this close to your dreams and then watching them brush past you like a stranger in the crowd."

—Burt Lancaster as Moonlight Graham

The Natural **(1984, baseball).**

"Pick me out a winner, Bobby."

—Robert Redford as Roy Hobbs, to the batboy

Bull Durham **(1988, baseball).**

"Don't think. It can only hurt the ball club."

—Kevin Costner as Crash Davis, to Nuke LaLoosh

North Dallas Forty **(1979, football).**

"I've been ignoring the fact that I'm falling apart."

—Nick Nolte as receiver Phil Elliott

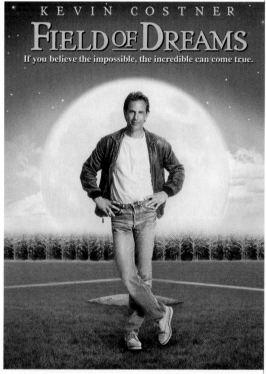

Hoosiers **(1986, basketball).** "If you put your effort and concentration into playing to your potential, to be the best that you can be, I don't care what the scoreboard says at the end of the game, in my book we're gonna be winners."

—Gene Hackman as Coach Norman Dale

A MIGHTY LONG GAME

CAL RIPKEN AND WADE BOGGS PLAY 33 INNINGS

It wasn't a good sign when a power failure delayed the start of the April 18, 1981, Rochester-Pawtucket game at McCoy Stadium by half an hour. The last thing anybody wanted on that cold Rhode Island night was a long night.

The first nine innings went fairly quickly, with the Red Wings taking a 1–0 lead into the bottom of the 9th. But the PawSox tied it up in the bottom of the inning, and the pitchers' duel continued . . . and continued . . . and continued. Finally, in the top of the 21st, Rochester pushed a run across, only to have Pawtucket third baseman Wade Boggs drive in the tying run in the bottom of the inning. And that's the way it stayed, knotted at 2–2, until International League president Harold Cooper suspended the game at 4:09 A.M. in the bottom of the 33rd.

It was agreed that the game would continue on June 23. When the two teams reconvened, Pawtucket scored the winning run in its first at bat when Dave Koza hit a bases-loaded single to knock in Marty Barrett. After the marathon slog in April, the final rally in June took all of 23 minutes. But the whole thing took 8 hours, 30 minutes, the longest professional game

Wade Boggs high-fives Marty Barrett as he scores the winning run two months later.

	1	2	3	4	5	6	7	8	9	10	11	12	13	14	15	16	17	18	19	20	21	22	23	24	25	26	27	28	29	30	31	32	33	R	H	E
RED WINGS	0	0	0	0	0	0	1	0	0	0	0	0	0	0	0	0	0	0	0	0	0	1	0	0	0	0	0	0	0	0	0	0	0	2	18	3
PAW SOX	0	0	0	0	0	0	0	1	0	0	0	0	0	0	0	0	0	0	0	1	0	0	0	0	0	0	0	0	0	0	0	0	1	3	21	1

in history. Said Pawtucket manager Joe Morgan, "I wanted to play another few innings, or seven to get to 40, so no one could ever break it."

Among the participants were two third basemen who ended up in the Hall of Fame, Boggs (4-for-12) and Cal Ripken Jr. (2-for-13); Jim Umbarger, who pitched 10 shutout innings for Rochester; and Bruce Hurst, who went five scoreless for the Sox. Recalled Hurst, "I remember striking out Ripken on a 3-and-2 breaking ball at 4 o'clock in the morning, and I don't think he ever forgave me."

The game—which attracted extra attention because it was played amid a strike by major league baseball players—produced a dozen other records, including those for the most putouts by a team (99, by Pawtucket), the most strikeouts by a team (34, by Rochester), and the most at bats by one team (114, by Pawtucket).

Unfortunately for Morgan, he wasn't on the bench when the winning run crossed the plate. He'd been ejected two months earlier, in the 21st or 22nd inning, for arguing about an interference call at first base.

The first notable author to write about baseball is none other than Jane Austen, who wrote this passage in the first chapter of *Northanger Abbey* in 1798:

". . . it was not very wonderful that Catherine, who had by nature nothing heroic about her, should prefer cricket, baseball, riding on horseback, and running about the country at the age of fourteen, to books . . ."

FAMOUS AMOS THE AMAZING MR. STAGG

His name is evoked every year for the Division III football championship, in Salem, Virginia, which is called the Stagg Bowl. But given the significance of his contributions to the game, they should name the Super Bowl after Amos Alonzo Stagg. As legendary Notre Dame coach Knute Rockne once said, "All football comes from Stagg."

The list of innovations Stagg introduced to the game is, well, staggering. It runs from the fundamental (the huddle, the tackling dummy, numbering plays and players, padding goalposts, awarding varsity letters) to the freewheeling (the end around, the lateral, the Statue of Liberty play, the man in motion). He is also credited with inventing the batting cage in baseball and the five-man formation for basketball. The mere mention of his name seemed to inspire people: The first atomic bomb was created underneath Stagg Stadium at the University of Chicago.

Stagg was born in West Orange, New Jersey, and attended Phillips Exeter Academy. From there, he went to Yale, where he was a divinity student, a member of Skull and Bones, the infamous secret society, and an end on the first-ever All-America football team. After deciding that his quiet manner would make him a poor preacher, Stagg devoted himself to sports—specifically, to football. He launched his coaching career in Massachusetts in 1890 at the School of Christian Workers, now Springfield College. In 1892, he became the head football coach at the University of Chicago and transformed the Maroons into one of the best teams in the nation. Once asked if a particular team was the best he had ever

> "If anything goes bad, I did it. If anything goes semi-good, we did it. If anything goes really good, then you did it. That's all it takes to get people to win football games for you.
> —Paul "Bear" Bryant

coached, Stagg replied, "I won't know that for another 20 years."

In 1932, he was forced out at Chicago because, at 70, he had reached retirement age. So he went on to the College of the Pacific, where he coached from 1933 to 1946, retiring as a full-time head coach at the age of 84. He later served as an assistant coach at California's Stockton Junior College and, with his son, at Pennsylvania's Susquehanna College. Throughout Stagg's career, his devoted wife was by his side, charting plays and feeding him statistics.

When he was 102 and living in a nursing home, a photographer who was taking his picture for a newspaper feature told him, "I hope I'm back here next year to take your photo." To which Stagg replied, "You look pretty healthy to me. I think you'll make it." Alas, Stagg died on March 17, 1965, five months shy of his 103rd birthday.

Amos Alonzo Stagg, 1928.

THE PUCK STOPS HERE WAYNE GRETZKY ON HOW TO TAPE A STICK

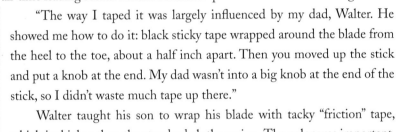

When Wayne Gretzky was a kid, taping his stick—or doing anything with his equipment, for that matter—was an almost-holy experience. "I remember spending so much time just looking at my skates and gloves, comparing them to what the pros were wearing," Gretzky says now.

Of course, the Great One didn't have your typical childhood. At 10, he became a household name in his native Canada after netting 378 goals in a single season, still an age-group record. Gretzky went on to become the NHL's all-time leading scorer. But his relationship with his stick never changed.

"The way I taped it was largely influenced by my dad, Walter. He showed me how to do it: black sticky tape wrapped around the blade from the heel to the toe, about a half inch apart. Then you moved up the stick and put a knob at the end. My dad wasn't into a big knob at the end of the stick, so I didn't waste much tape up there."

Walter taught his son to wrap his blade with tacky "friction" tape, which is thicker than the standard cloth version. The color was important, too: Black tape helps disguise the black puck, making it harder for goalies to pick up lightning-quick snap shots.

Gretzky added one refinement all his own. "The last thing I did was put some baby powder on the blade to relieve some of the tape's stickiness," he says. "I always felt the baby powder gave me a smoother surface so I could feel the puck better."

Now head coach of the Phoenix Coyotes and the father of three hockey players, Gretzky says that he sees guys spending lots of time bending, taping, even blowtorching their sticks—time that might be better spent on the ice.

"I don't think I spent an inordinate amount of time on my sticks," Gretzky says. "I believed that as long as I put the time into practicing hard, what I did preparing my stick would become secondary."

> "I skate to where the puck is going to be, not to where it has been."
> —Wayne Gretzky

26 Wayne Gretzky on How to Tape a Stick

GLASS CEILING THE FIRST FEMALE DUNK

Candace Parker does it all the time now. But who exactly was the first woman to dunk a basketball?

If you answered Lisa Leslie, sorry. She was the first player to do it in a WNBA game, in 2002. The correct answer is Georgeann Wells, who dunked while playing for West Virginia University against the University of Charleston on December 21, 1984—nine days before LeBron James was born.

It happened before a small crowd in a tiny gym in Elkins, West Virginia, and unfortunately there were no television cameras to capture the feat. The 6-foot-7 sophomore had been dunking in practice, and as Wells (now Wells-Blackwell) recalls, she was warming up before the second half when point guard Lisa Ribble said, "I feel it tonight. Do you?" Wells replied, "I feel sick to my stomach."

But with 11:18 left to play and the Lady Mountaineers ahead by a comfortable margin, Ribble lofted a long pass to Wells, who took a couple of steps and then dunked it with one hand. Keep in mind that back then, women played with a men's regulation-size ball, not the smaller ball used in the women's game today. A later dunk against Xavier University was captured on film, and the Naismith Memorial Basketball Hall of Fame, in Springfield, Massachusetts, chronicled Wells's feat in a special display.

Wells-Blackwell, however, doesn't think a woman dunking is a big deal. "My thing is just Why not slam? Do it because you can."

Georgeann Wells dunks for the Mountaineers.

You know him as Dikembe Mutombo, but at birth, in Zaire, he was named Dikembe Mutombo Mpolondo Mukamba Jean Jacque Wamutombo.

BREAKFAST OF CHAMPION
A BREAKDOWN OF MICHAEL PHELPS'S MORNING MEAL

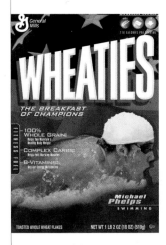

For the record, this is what Michael Phelps eats in the morning when he's competing:

- three fried-egg sandwiches with cheese, lettuce, tomatoes, fried onions, and mayonnaise
- a five-egg omelet
- a bowl of grits
- three slices of french toast with powdered sugar
- three chocolate-chip pancakes
- two cups of coffee

That's approximately 4,000 calories, not counting the other swimmers he seems to eat for breakfast.

But you're not Michael Phelps. What should a normal athletic person have for breakfast? Let's ask Michelle Daum, M.S., R.D., a pediatric and adult nutritionist in Westchester County, New York.

First of all, I'm in awe of what Michael Phelps eats. Talk about power breakfasts. Good for him—but not for the rest of us. Unless you're going to swim in eight Olympic events in a week, it's not the way to start your day.

What you really want for breakfast is whole grains, fruits or vegetables, and a source of protein, i.e., eggs, nuts, cheese, or milk. I didn't notice any fruits in Michael's breakfast, and he could do without the mayonnaise, chocolate chips, and butter they must have used to cook all that. Would you like to hear about some of the breakfasts I give my kids?"

Sure.

Monday. Calcium-fortified orange juice, yogurt with sliced bananas, granola
Tuesday. Sliced melon, whole-grain cereal, glass of low-fat milk
Wednesday. Bagel with a slice of Muenster, apple with peanut butter, glass of low-fat milk
Thursday. Orange juice, oatmeal with almonds and raisins
Friday. Two scrambled egg whites, grapes, glass of low-fat milk, whole-wheat English muffins.

How about Wheaties? Says Daum, "Add some raisins, don't add sugar, pour on low-fat milk, and it actually could be the Breakfast of Champions."

CHAMPION OF BREAKFAST HOW WHEATIES GOT THAT SLOGAN

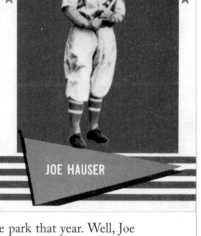

JOE HAUSER

Phelps is just one of about 1,500 athletes who have appeared on a box of Wheaties since 1933, when Babe Ruth became the first. That was also the year the famous slogan was invented. It seems that General Mills had decided to spoon out $10,000 for the broadcast rights to the baseball games of the hometown Minneapolis Millers, and included in those rights was a billboard in center field of Nicollet Park. A representative of the Millers asked Knox Reeves, the advertising man for Wheaties, what should be put on the sign. Reeves, seated behind his desk, doodled a cereal box on a piece of paper and wrote down the fateful words: "Wheaties—Breakfast of Champions."

As it happened, Wheaties also offered a case of the cereal to any Miller who hit a home run in the home park that year. Well, Joe Hauser chose that season to hit 69 homers, 33 of them in Nicollet Park. That meant 33 cases, or 792 boxes, for Hauser. Some 50 years later, Hauser recalled, "I gave most of them to my teammates. Not that I didn't like them—I still eat Wheaties."

Ruth was once asked on a radio show to push a Wheaties cookie that mothers could bake for their kids. His line was supposed to be "And so, boys and girls, don't forget to tell your mother to buy Wheaties so she can make these cookies." But in rehearsal, he kept pronouncing *cookies* "kookies." He promised he would get the word right when the time came, but sure enough, he got it wrong while he was on the air. After a moment of silence, Ruth told the audience, "I'm a son of a bitch if I didn't say koo-kies again."

"Champions get many a small boy to eat a good breakfast!"

Betty Crocker

How Wheaties Got That Slogan **2 9**

GLOVE AFFAIR
OMAR VIZQUEL ON HOW TO BREAK IN A MITT

You can spend almost as much money on products for breaking in a baseball glove as you can for the mitt itself: oils, foams, molds, straps, even oven-activated potions. You can, as some major leaguers have done, throw a new glove in a whirlpool or run over it with your car.

But take it from 11-time Gold Glove–winner Omar Vizquel. All you really have to do with a new glove is play with it. "I don't do too much to a new glove," says Vizquel, who has played more games at shortstop than anyone else in major league history. "I take it out to the field in batting practice, take ground balls with it, play catch with it. Gloves take their own shape, and the shape you want is the shape of your hand."

To break in a glove, Vizquel will bend the fingers down toward the palm, but that's the way of infielders. Outfielders prefer a more vertical pocket, so they bend the fingers thumb to pinkie. Either way, it takes a little time and a lot of play.

Most major leaguers have several mitts in rotation: a game glove, a replacement, some that they like that aren't quite ready for graduation. Vizquel has had the same gamer for three years, so he has a number of gloves figuratively chomping at the bit. "Sometimes I'll give one to a friend," he says. "But he's got to be a real friend. And he'd better take very good care of it."

Too much oil makes a glove heavy. Those oven potions will turn your laces into french fries. If you still insist on slathering something on your glove, any shaving cream with lanolin will do. (Little Leaguers can have fun with that.) And when baseball season is over, you might want to spread a light coat of petroleum jelly on the glove and put it in an unsealed plastic bag.

But basically, the key to breaking in a glove is provided by the umpire before every game: **Play ball!**

> **The number of baseball gloves produced from the hide of one cow is four or five.**

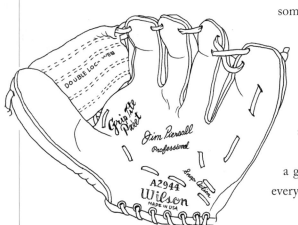

NET RESULT

ON THE ORIGINS OF CUTTING DOWN THE NET

T he popular tradition of cutting down the nets after a big basketball victory can be traced to one man, legendary North Carolina State coach Everett Case. According to the historian Matt Zeysing at the Basketball Hall of Fame, the Old Grey Fox was the first person to cut down a net, snipping it off as his Wolfpack held him aloft after the team won the Southern Conference championship in 1947. He simply wanted the net as a souvenir of the victory.

Should you be so lucky as to earn a similar distinction, please keep these recommendations in mind:

1. Use a ladder. Riding on someone's shoulders while holding scissors is dangerous.
2. Borrow the trainer's tape cutters to do the honors.
3. Don't get hung up on the order of doing the cutting, but make sure the team captains and the coach go last.
4. The team may choose to let individual players cut off little pieces of cord for themselves, but if the players instead clip each of the hooked cords and thus preserve the net, they'll have a much better photo op when the net is twirled around or worn around the neck.

Everett Case cutting down the net in 1959.

> **"If you make every game a life-and-death thing, you're going to have problems. You'll be dead a lot."**
> —former North Carolina basketball coach Dean Smith

JIMMY V

Another North Carolina State basketball coach who cut down the nets, Jim Valvano, gave a beautiful and moving speech at the 1993 ESPY awards. Dying of cancer, Valvano famously said, "Don't give up; don't ever give up." But Valvano was as much about laughter as he was about tears, and he brought down the house that night with this story:

I have to remember the first speech I ever gave. I was coaching at Rutgers University, that was my first job . . . and I was the freshman coach. . . . My idol as a coach was Vince Lombardi, and I read this book called *Commitment to Excellence* by Vince Lombardi. And in the book, Lombardi talked about the first time he spoke before his Green Bay Packer team in the locker room—they were perennial losers. . . . Three minutes before they could take the field, Lombardi comes in, bangs the door open, . . . walked back and forth, like this, just walked, staring at the players. . . . "Gentlemen, we will be successful this year if you can focus on three things and three things only: your family, your religion, and the Green Bay Packers." . . . They knocked the walls down and the rest was history.

I said, that's beautiful. I'm going to do that. Your family, your religion, and Rutgers basketball. That's it. I had it. Listen, I'm 21 years old. The kids I'm coaching are 19, . . . and I'm going to be the greatest coach in the world, the next Lombardi. . . .

I'm practicing outside of the locker room and the managers tell me you got to go in. Not yet, not yet. Family, religion, Rutgers basketball. All eyes on me. I got it, I got it. Then finally they said, "three minutes." I said, "Fine." True story. I go to knock the doors open just like Lombardi. Boom! They don't open. I almost broke my arm. . . . Now I was down, the players were looking. Help the coach out, help him out. Now I did like Lombardi. I walked back and forth, and I was going like that with my arm, getting the feeling back in it. Finally I said, "Gentlemen, all eyes on me." These kids wanted to play, they're 19. . . . "Gentlemen, we'll be successful this year if you can focus on three things and three things only: your family, your religion, and the Green Bay Packers," I told them. I did that. I remember that.

I remember, I remember where I came from.

> "Go for the moon. If you don't get it, you'll still be heading for a star."
>
> —NBA Hall of Famer Willis Reed

> "One day of practice is like one day of clean living. It doesn't do you any good."
>
> —Hall of Fame basketball coach Abe Lemons

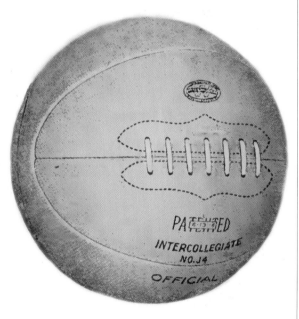

> The only player ever to win both an NCAA basketball championship and a World Series is Tim Stoddard, who was a member of the 1974 North Carolina State Wolfpack and the 1979 Baltimore Orioles.

When did the practice of giving athletes nicknames start? Well, actually it dates back to ancient Greece and a wrestler named Sostratus of Sicyon. Because he could defeat opponents simply by bending back their fingers until they gave up, he became known as Acrochersites, or "Fingerer."

Since then, we've had the Toe (Lou Groza), Crazylegs (Elroy Hirsch), and Cabeza (Tony Fernandez). In fact, we've had athletes named after animals (Hippo Vaughn), vegetables (Spinach Melillo), and minerals (Clint "Scrap Iron" Courtney).

The list is endless and mind-boggling. To encapsulate the richness and creativity of nicknames, we've created this quiz, in which we ask you to match 26 nicknames with their owners. If you get all 26, call yourself the Professor (Jim Brosnan):

Ted Williams, 1957.

> "I think about baseball when I wake up in the morning. I think about it all day and I dream about it at night. The only time I don't think about it is when I'm playing it."
>
> —Hall of Famer Carl Yastrzemski

1. Bambi
2. Thumper
3. Mongoose
4. Snake
5. Little Poison
6. Big Dipper
7. Moon
8. Eclipse
9. Astronaut
10. Poet
11. Gulliver
12. Chaucer
13. Flying Housewife
14. Grandmother
15. Godfather
16. Hitman
17. Thin Man
18. Spider-Man
19. Batman
20. Clark Kent
21. Lincoln Locomotive
22. Pullman
23. Suitcase
24. American Tourister
25. Boxing Bellhop
26. Pitchin' Mortician

A. DeWayne Scales
B. Fanny Blankers-Koen
C. Leo Lewis
D. Red Rocha
E. Paul Lehner
F. Waite Hoyt
G. James Donaldson
H. Ted Williams
I. Kurt Rambis
J. Harry Simpson
K. Lance Alworth
L. Kenny Stabler
M. Philip Powers
N. Wilt Chamberlain
O. Eddie Lukon
P. Anthony Hallahan
Q. Lloyd Waner
R. Benny Ayala
S. Fred Apostoli
T. Tommy Lasorda
U. Andre Rison
V. Ed Charles
W. Edwin Elliot
X. Thomas Hearns
Y. Andrew Porter
Z. Richard Wood

Lance Alworth, 1970.

Key: 1-K, 2-H, 3-O, 4-L, 5-Q, 6-N, 7-P, 8-R, 9-A, 10-V, 11-E, 12-W, 13-B, 14-M, 15-T, 16-X, 17-D, 18-U, 19-Z, 20-I, 21-C, 22-Y, 23-J, 24-G, 25-S, 26-F

SIGN LANGUAGE

Have you ever marveled at the communications technique of a third base coach, ever wondered why he has to touch so many different parts of his body and uniform to send the batter the right message? Rich Donnelly, a third base coach for five teams during his long career, unlocks the mystery:

You have a bunt sign, a take sign, a steal sign, and a hit-and-run sign—to name a few—and each one of those signs is a touch. There are basically 12 areas you can touch without going to jail. What I try to do is touch all those spots at least once, giving the sign in the middle. You don't want to go too fast or too slow.

Let's say that the bunt sign is the right hand off the hat. I tell the players to just look at my hat. Don't look at my ears, nose, or face; don't try to follow my hands, just concentrate on the hat. I try to keep it simple: If I spit, the hit-and-run is on. If I take my foot and tap it on the ground, maybe something else is on. I also use claps—give all my signs and clap once, which means the bunt is on.

You don't want the other team stealing your signs, so different players have different sets of signs, and you have to change them up when a player gets traded.

The number one mistake coaches make is bad tempo, changing speeds if something is on. You can tell. You can also sometimes see a coach's eyes light up when something is on. The other team is always watching your signs and may even be filming you.

When I was in Pittsburgh, Jim Leyland had the trainer give the steal sign by folding his arms across his chest. One night, we had a very slow guy on first, but it was so cold that the trainer crossed his arms to stay warm. The runner was out by a mile.

I love the job. It's like a chess game. I practice my signs at a red light—I'm putting on the squeeze and the guy in the car next to me is like, "What the heck are you doing?" I practice them in the mirror at home. I have eight kids, and I used to tell them and my wife, "See if you can pick up my sign," then go really fast.

In church, people think I'm blessing myself. I'm not, I'm giving the sign for a hit-and-run.

At the end of the 1953 season, Major League Baseball banned the players' common practice of leaving their gloves on the field while their team batted. Among the complainants was Yankee manager Casey Stengel, who said, "We are trying every which way to speed up games. Now we have a rule that makes for delays."

FOR PETE'S SAKE
THE DAY A CLUBHOUSE GUY SCORED A TOUCHDOWN

"PETE" SHEEHY

YANKEE EQUIPMENT MANAGER
1927 - 1985

KEEPER OF THE PINSTRIPES

The life of a locker-room attendant is not easy. Sure, there's the reflected glory of working with famous players for a famous team, but mostly it's drudgery: doing laundry, shining shoes, cleaning up messes, packing and unpacking . . .

Pete Sheehy did it for 58 years at Yankee Stadium for the New York Yankees and the New York football Giants. One day, though, he actually got credit for a victory. The day was November 12, 1961, and the credit came from Allie Sherman, the Giants' head coach:

I'm sitting at my desk in Yankee Stadium, drawing up my game plan for the Eagles game that week, and Pete is pushing a broom. I say to no one in particular, "I wish we had some speed." Pete goes on sweeping and pipes up, "You do." I say, "I do?" He says, "Yeah—on defense." So I draw up these plays designed to take advantage of Erich Barnes and Jimmy Patton, defensive backs, but our two fastest guys.

Sure enough, in the second quarter, Sherman sent in Barnes and Patton. And Y. A. Tittle threw a 62-yard touchdown pass to Barnes that put the Giants ahead 24–7 and propelled them to a 38–21 victory. After the game, Sherman told the reporters whom he had gotten the idea from.

"Now it's Monday morning," said Sherman, "and I'm back in the office. But my coffee isn't there. Pete always brought me my coffee. Never missed a day. So I ask around, a little worried about Pete. And they tell me he couldn't come in that morning. Turns out he was on the *Today* show, talking about how he won the game against the Eagles."

> **Because of a shortage of players due to World War II, the Philadelphia Eagles and Pittsburgh Steelers put together a combined team in 1943 called the "Steagles" that finished the season 5-4-1.**

JUST FOR KICKS
LANDON DONOVAN ON HOW TO SCORE ON A PK

A penalty kick in soccer seems fairly easy: The shooter steps up to a ball placed 12 yards from a goal that's 24 feet wide and 8 feet high, with only a goalie in between. As difficult as it is to score a goal in soccer, the success rate for potting penalties is roughly 80 percent. According to Landon Donovan, the U.S. national team's all-time leading scorer, "The ideal approach is to focus on the corner you want to put the ball in and hit it hard. If you hit it properly, the goalie's not going to save it—most of the time."

Ah, while Donovan is a perfect 8-for-8 on PKs in international play, there are other stars—namely, Roberto Baggio and David Beckham—who have missed penalty kicks that would have given their teams important victories. A poorly taken spot kick can actually send an entire nation into mourning, not to mention your local rec team.

Donovan has some advice for penalty kickers everywhere: "As you get better at it, you figure out how to keep the goalie from knowing what side you're going to. You don't ever want to look where you are hitting it or make it too obvious by standing on one side of the ball. The more hidden you are with your body language, the harder it is to predict where the ball will go. You want to keep the goalie guessing."

Donovan also notes that you don't necessarily have to shoot for the corners. "In a big game, a lot of times it's best to shoot right down the middle. The keeper is probably going to anticipate hard and dive in one direction or the other. It's risky, but when it goes in, you're the hero."

MIGHTIEST FIGHT (BOXING)
THE FIRST ALI-FRAZIER BOUT

For all the the great boxing matches in history, there is one that stands above the rest, at least for the people who saw Muhammad Ali fight Joe Frazier in Madison Square Garden on March 8, 1971. The setup itself promised remembrance: boxer versus puncher, brash versus taciturn, counterculture versus establishment, undefeated versus undefeated. And there was this: It was Ali's first big fight since being stripped of the heavyweight title in 1967 for refusing to accept induction into the U.S. Army on religious grounds.

As usual, Ali heralded the fight with a poem: "Joe's gonna come out smokin' / But I ain't gonna be jokin' / I'll be pickin' and pokin' / Pouring water on his smokin' / This might shock and amaze ya / But I'm gonna destroy Joe Frazier."

Covering the fight for Ali's hometown Louisville *Courier-Journal* was Dave Kindred, who wrote, "I don't remember breathing all night long. Even with Frazier pounding on him early in the fight, Ali leaned back against the ring ropes and made eye contact with us at ringside, calling out, 'No contest, nooooo contest.'"

But it was a contest, 15 rounds of brains and brawn, heart and soul. Ali was behind on most cards, but he never seemed more noble. He had been pummeled mercilessly by Frazier, but he handed out his own punishment. When the bell rang for the 15th and final round, out staggered Ali in his red trunks, exhausted but proud, and Frazier in his green trunks, eyes swollen shut but determined. Here's the ringside call by legendary announcer Don Dunphy:

Referee Arthur Mercante has them touch gloves, something they've been doing all night. . . . Muhammad Ali's going to go boxing again . . . and Frazier goes back to the attack. . . . Step back, says the referee, . . . time is important here. . . . [Crowd roars with 2:42 left in the round as a Frazier left hook puts Ali on the canvas,

"If you screw things up in tennis, it's 15-love. If you screw up in boxing, it's your ass."
—boxer Randall "Tex" Cobb

sending the tassels on his sneakers flying.] . . . He takes the mandatory eight count, the only knockdown of the fight. . . . Muhammad Ali was flat on his back, but he's a well-conditioned athlete, . . . however, he's real tired. . . . Frazier smartly goes for the body and Muhammad Ali covers up, . . . two minutes to go in the fight, two minutes, . . . the crowd, needless to say, is in a bedlam. . . . Oh! What a shot! If Joe had followed that up, he would've finished him. . . . Muhammad Ali has never taken such a battering. . . . Frazier is just touch-shadowing him now, . . . one minute, one minute left, look for a last-minute flurry from Muhammad Ali, . . . less than a minute to go. . . . Muhammad Ali gamely fights back . . . and Ali again makes the clinch. . . . Remember, the scoring is on a rounds basis,

Ali and Frazier square off at Madison Square Garden on March 8, 1971.

Frazier is tired and his eyes are closing, . . . half a minute, half a minute to go, Frazier won the big rounds, the 11th and the 15th, at least up to now. . . . Frazier has the man in the corner, . . . 10 seconds . . . 5 seconds. . . . We'll have an interview with the winner, and maybe with the loser.

The winner was Frazier, on all three cards. But Ali emerged as a more heroic figure. Said his ringside doctor, Ferdie Pacheco, "That night he was the most courageous fighter I'd ever seen. He was going to get up if he was dead." Somehow that night, the Greatest became even greater.

BRAZIL NUTS

YOU, TOO, CAN HAVE A
BRAZILIAN SOCCER NAME

His name is actually **Edson Arantes do Nascimento,** but the world knows him as Pelé. Millions wear the jersey of Ricardo Izecson dos Santos Leite, aka Kaká. Part of the allure of Brazilian soccer is the poetic kick of its nicknames. Indeed, 21 of the 30 Brazilians on the roster for the 2010 World Cup are known by just one name.

Why is that? As a consequence of its history of slavery and poverty, Brazil still has one of the lowest literacy rates in the world, so simple, short childhood names are the norm. (Even the president, Luiz Inacio Lula da Silva, answers to Lula.) The mellifluous Portuguese language also helps: Because Ronaldo Luis Nazário de Lima came on the world soccer stage first, he gets to be called Ronaldo. When Ronaldo de Assis Moreira came along, he became Ronaldinho, or "Little Ronaldo."

So what if you're not Brazilian but you want a Brazilian soccer name? You could go traditional and simply use your first name or a childhood nickname. Or you could go online, to a website called minimalsworld .net, click on the Brazilian soccername generator ("BrazilName") and enter your first and last names, as well as your favorite jersey number. In seconds, you'll see your name emblazoned on a gold and green jersey. Say your name is Landon Donovan and your number is 10. Presto, you're Donovisco.

> **"Enthusiasm is everything. It must be taut and vibrating like a guitar string."**
> —Pelé

BY THE NUMBERS

HOWIE SCHWAB COUNTS UP THE UNIFORMS

If you've ever seen the game show *Stump the Schwab,* on ESPN, you know that the network's chief researcher, Howie Schwab, has an encyclopedic grasp of sports. You also know that he has an endless supply of jerseys. So we asked Howie to give us his favorite uniform numbers from 1 to 100. Naturally, he didn't stop there:

0   **George Plimpton:** His number in *Paper Lion.*
     Sorry, Al Oliver and Gilbert Arenas.

00   **Robert Parrish:** Played a record 21 years in the NBA. (Jim
     Otto, Jack Clark.)

09   **Benito Santiago:** He caught for 10 different major league teams.

⅛   **Eddie Gaedel:** The midget who batted for
     Bill Veeck's St. Louis Browns.

1   **Oscar Robertson:** Big O also wore 14, but
     he's the *one.* (Warren Moon, Ozzie Smith.)

1A   **Secretariat:** That's what he wore in the
     Kentucky Derby.

1½   **Robert Merrill:** The number given by the Yankees
     to their favorite baritone.

2   **Derek Jeter:** My wife would kill me if I didn't pick
     him. (Moses Malone, Brad Park.)

3   **Babe Ruth:** No argument here. (Allen Iverson,
     Dales Earnhardt and Murphy.)

4   **Lou Gehrig:** The first number to be retired.
     (Bobby Orr, Brett Favre.)

5   **Joe DiMaggio:** The best of a lot of great fins.
     (Johnny Bench, George Brett.)

6   **Bill Russell:** Personified winning. (Dr. J, Stan the Man.)

7   **Mickey Mantle:** Last of the Yankees for a while. (John Elway,
     Phil Esposito.)

"I just wrap my arms around the whole backfield and peel 'em one by one until I get to the ball carrier. Him I keep."

—Gene "Big Daddy" Lipscomb

8   **Cal Ripken Jr.:** Actually, the number is 2,632. (Yogi, Yaz, Steve Young.)

9   **Ted Williams:** The greatest hitter ever. (Gordie Howe, Maurice Richard, Mia Hamm.)

10 **Pelé:** A bow to the world's most popular sport. (Walt Frazier, Fran Tarkenton.)

11 **Mark Messier:** The Rangers' cup belongs to him. (Phil Simms, Carl Hubbell.)

12 **Terry Bradshaw:** A passer's number, worn by Joe Namath, Tom Brady, *and* John Stockton.

13 **Wilt Chamberlain:** Still casts a long shadow. (A-Rod, Dan Marino, Steve Nash.)

14 **Pete Rose:** Hey, this isn't Cooperstown. (Bob Cousy, Otto Graham, Ernie Banks.)

15 **Bart Starr:** The original Super Bowl winner. (Thurman Munson, Earl Monroe.)

16 **Joe Montana:** As classy as they come. (Bobby Clarke, Whitey Ford, Bob Lanier.)

17 **John Havlicek:** He stole the ball, and the number from Dizzy Dean.

18 **Peyton Manning:** The first of two Colt QB greats. (Darryl Strawberry.)

19 **Johnny Unitas:** The second. (Bob Feller, Willis Reed, Steve Yzerman.)

20 **Barry Sanders:** Little Big Man. (Mike Schmidt, Lou Brock, Frank Robinson.)

21 **Roberto Clemente:** MLB should retire his number, too. (KG, Rocket, Warren Spahn.)

22 **Emmitt Smith:** Nobody could catch 22. (Elgin Baylor, Jim Palmer, Mike Bossy.)

23 **Michael Jordan:** As much a lock as Ruth. (LeBron James, Don Mattingly.)

24 **Willie Mays:** Hey, who else? (Bill Bradley, Ken Griffey Jr., Kobe Bryant.)

25 **Barry Bonds:** Ironically, his main competition is Mark McGwire.

26 **Wade Boggs:** Led the league in hitting five times. (Billy Williams, Herb Adderley.)

27 **Carlton Fisk:** Pudge's Red Sox number. (Juan Marichal, Catfish Hunter.)

28 **Marshall Faulk:** His versatility was unmatched. (Darrell Green, Willie Gallimore.)

29 **Ken Dryden:** Montreal's great net minder. (Eric Dickerson, Satchel Paige.)

30 **Nolan Ryan:** Spell his name with 5,714 *K*s. (Ken Griffey Jr., Martin Brodeur.)

31 **Dave Winfield:** An NBA and NFL draftee as well. (Reggie Miller, Greg Maddux.)

32 **Jim Brown:** Over some other amazing 32s: Magic, Koufax, Carlton, Walton.

Which 32 would you choose?

33   **Kareem Abdul-Jabbar:** Another tough call. (Larry Bird, Sammy Baugh.)

34   **Walter Payton:** Left us all too soon. (Charles Barkley, Bo Jackson.)

35   **Frank Thomas:** A surefire Hall of Famer. (Phil Niekro, Alan Ameche.)

36   **Gaylord Perry:** Cy Young winner in both leagues. (Marion Motley, Robin Roberts.)

37   **Doak Walker:** Hey, he has his own award. (Casey Stengel, Lester Hayes.)

38   **George Rogers:** Heisman winner and NFL workhorse. (Curt Schilling.)

39   **Roy Campanella:** 142 RBIs for the '53 Dodgers. (Larry Csonka, Dominik Hasek.)

40   **Gale Sayers:** More than a character in *Brian's Song*. (Pat Tillman, Bill Laimbeer.)

41   **Tom Seaver:** A number that symbolized determination. (Wes Unseld, Brian Piccolo.)

42   **Jackie Robinson:** The first—and foremost. (Sid Luckman, Nate Thurmond.)

43   **Richard Petty:** Long live the King. (Dennis Eckersley, Brad Daugherty.)

44   **Hank Aaron:** Long live the one-time Home Run King. (Jerry West, Reggie Jackson.)

45   **Bob Gibson:** Hard to believe that 1.16 ERA in '68. (Archie Griffin, Pedro Martinez.)

46   **Andy Pettitte:** Haven't had a Yankee for a while. (Lee Smith, Chuck Muncie.)

47   **Tom Glavine:** Always in control. (Mel Blount, Jack Morris.)

48   **Lee Smith:** Just one of this closer's many numbers. (Torii Hunter, Moose Johnston.)

49   **Ron Guidry:** It's not a Yankee thing—honest. (Tim Wakefield, Tom Landry.)

50   **David Robinson:** Athlete, officer, and gentleman. (Rebecca Lobo, Mike Singletary.)

51   **Dick Butkus:** The twentieth-century QB's nightmare. (Randy Johnson, Ichiro Suzuki.)

52   **Ray Lewis:** The twenty-first-century QB's nightmare. (Mike Webster, C. C. Sabathia.)

53   **Don Drysdale:** Wed a Hall of Famer, Ann Meyers. (Harry Carson, Artis Gilmore.)

54   **Goose Gossage:** Took him too long to get to Cooperstown. (Brian Urlacher.)

> **Eddie Gaedel, the 3-foot-7 pinch hitter whom Bill Veeck sent up to bat for the St. Louis Browns in 1951, made another appearance for Veeck, in 1959—as one of the "Martians" who captured the White Sox' diminutive double-play combination, Luis Aparicio and Nellie Fox.**

> **The puck that Maurice Richard scored to set the all-time NHL record for goals in 1952 (325 at the time) is actually in the possession of Queen Elizabeth II, who was a fan.**

55 Orel Hershiser: 59 consecutive scoreless innings. (Junior Seau, Dikembe Mutombo.)

56 Lawrence Taylor: Kept offensive coordinators up nights. (Mark Buehrle.)

57 Johan Santana: Two Cy Youngs and counting. (Tom Jackson, Dwight Stephenson.)

58 Jack Lambert: The first of two great Steeler LBs named Jack. (Jonathan Papelbon.)

59 Jack Ham: The second. (London Fletcher, Donnie Edwards.)

60 Chuck Bednarik: Last of the two-way linemen. (Tommy Nobis, Otto Graham.)

61 Curley Culp: Loved those Raiders-Chiefs games—and this KC DT. (Bill George.)

62 Jim Langer: The perfect center for the perfect Dolphins. (Ed White.)

63 Willie Lanier: He was right there behind Culp. (Gene Upshaw, Lee Roy Selmon.)

64 Jerry Kramer: Dick Schaap wrote books about him. (Jack Reynolds, Dave Wilcox.)

65 Gary Zimmerman: Blocked for Steve Young in the USFL. (Elvin Bethea, Tom Mack.)

66 Mario Lemieux: The center who saved Pittsburgh. (Ray Nitschke, Larry Little.)

67 Reggie McKenzie: Let's give it up for Buffalo's Electric Company. (Art Still.)

68 Jaromir Jagr: A near equal to Lemieux with the Penguins. (L. C. Greenwood.)

69 Mark Schlereth: Stink had almost that many knee surgeries. (Tim Krumrie.)

70 Jim Marshall: Did more than run the wrong way. (Sam Huff, Rayfield Wright.)

> **The winner of the 3000-meter steeplechase in the 1952 Helsinki Olympics was 29-year-old FBI agent Horace Ashenfelter, who trained at night in Glen Ridge, New Jersey, by running over park benches.**

"There is among us a far closer relationship than the purely social one of a fraternal organization because we are bound together not only by a single interest but by a common goal. To win. Nothing else matters, and nothing else will do."
—Sandy Koufax

> **"You spend a good piece of your life gripping a baseball and in the end it turns out that it was the other way around all the time."**
> —Jim Bouton

71 **Tony Boselli:** The epitome of the right offensive tackle. (Alex Karras, Fred Dean.)

72 **Carlton Fisk:** A double play—Pudge's White Sox number. (Ed Jones, William Perry.)

73 **John Hannah:** *SI* called him "the best offensive lineman of all time." (Joe Klecko.)

74 **Bob Lilly:** He spelled Doomsday for Dallas. (Merlin Olsen, Ron Mix.)

75 **Mean Joe Greene:** That Coke commercial still gets to me. (Howie Long, Barry Zito.)

76 **Lou Groza:** The Toe! (Rosey Grier, Marion Motley.)

77 **Red Grange:** The Galloping Ghost! (Ray Bourque, Jim Parker.)

78 **Anthony Muñoz:** Great number for the trenches. (Art Shell, Bruce Smith, and Bubba Smith.)

79 **Bob St. Clair:** Impressive Canton credentials. (Harvey Martin, Rosey Brown.)

80 **Jerry Rice:** Greatest receiver of all time. (Cris Carter, Kellen Winslow.)

81 **Tim Brown:** Favorite of an amazing WR group. (TO, Randy Moss, Art Monk.)

82 **Raymond Berry:** Old-school, I know, but there's nobody smarter. (John Stallworth.)

83 **Andre Reed:** Very underrated receiver. (Ted Hendricks, Mark Clayton.)

84 **Shannon Sharpe:** A tight end who had to be double teamed. (White Shoes Johnson.)

85 **Jack Youngblood:** Give me a guy who'll play hurt. (Max McGee, Nick Buoniconti.)

86 **Buck Buchanan:** More love for those old Chiefs. (Gary Collins, Hines Ward.)

87 **Sidney Crosby:** Born on 8/7/87, born to score. (Willie Davis, Dwight Clark.)

88 **Lynn Swann:** The grace of Swann over the swagger of Michael Irvin.

89 **Mike Ditka:** How many guys are immortalized in an *SNL* skit? (Gino Marchetti.)

90 **Bob Kurland:** A giant of college hoops at Oklahoma A&M. (George Webster.)

Eleanor Holm, who won the gold medal in the 100-meter backstroke at the 1932 Los Angeles Games, was expelled from the 1936 U.S. Olympic team because of her misbehavior (drinking, shooting craps, obscenity) aboard the SS *Manhattan* on its voyage to the games in Berlin.

91   Dennis Rodman: *Bad As I Wanna Be,* but great as a rebounder. (Sergei Fedorov.)

92   Reggie White: The Minister of Defense left us way too soon. (Michael Strahan.)

93   Doug Gilmour: Drove hockey opponents crazy. (Dwight Freeney, Gilbert Brown.)

94   Charles Haley: A true champion—five Super Bowl rings. (Kabeer Gbaja-Biamila.)

95   Richard Dent: Driving force on the '85 Bears D. (Chad Hennings, Chris Hovan.)

96   Clyde Simmons: 15 seasons as a DE in the NFL. (Pavel Bure, Cortez Kennedy.)

97   Cornelius Bennett: Beloved in Tuscaloosa and Buffalo. (Jeremy Roenick.)

98   Tom Harmon: Heisman winner at Michigan and a fine broadcaster. (Tony Siragusa.)

99   Wayne Gretzky: The Greatest One. (George Mikan, Warren Sapp, Manny Ramirez.)

207   Tommie Smith: That's the number he was wearing when he raised his fist in '68.

After Stella Walsh, the sprinter who won the 100-meter gold medal in the 1932 Olympics, was killed in 1980 by a stray bullet at a Cleveland shopping center, an autopsy revealed that she was actually a man.

At the 2006 NBA All-Star Jam Session, in Houston, Joseph Odhiambo spun a basketball on his finger for a world-record 4 hours, 15 minutes.

FIELD DAY

"A champion is afraid of losing. Everyone else is afraid of winning."
—Billie Jean King

BILL OF RIGHTS

THE ORIOLES ON HOW TO WEAR YOUR BB CAP

Baseball caps are nearly as old as the game itself: The New York Knickerbockers, the very first organized team, wore them to prevent sunburn and provide shade. They're nevertheless subject to fashion. Indeed, you can tell a lot about a person by the bill of his (or her) cap: curved or straight; frontward, backward, or askew. Among actual baseball players nowadays, there's the old-school crescent bill and the new-school flat bill. Oriole second baseman Brian Roberts, who's a traditionalist, molds the bill of his 100 percent wool cap by (1) dipping it in water, (2) zapping it in a microwave for 20 seconds, and (3) rolling the brim in his palms a couple of dozen times before heading out to play.

There are other variations of the water-heat torture method, some involving dishwashers and ovens, but the basic idea is to make the cardboard inside the brim more malleable. To get just the right arch, you can also jam the bill into a coffee cup and leave it overnight or wrap it around a hair spray bottle and secure it with rubber bands.

Upholding tradition: Brian Roberts.

The Cleveland Indians, named after Penobscot Indian Louis Sockalexis, have had five other Native American players: Virgil Cheeves (Cherokee), Jesse Petty (Cherokee), Ike Kahdot (Potowatomie), Cal McLish (Choctaw), and Allie Reynolds (Muskogee).

5 0   BILL OF RIGHTS

> **"Holy Father, do you realize that you and I are both former Cardinals?"**
> —Ducky Medwick, upon meeting Pope Pius XII

The flat visor, however, has become more and more popular since being introduced to mainstream baseball by the Harlem entry in the 2002 Little League World Series. Oriole closer George Sherrill rocks a corpse-stiff brim, which he preserves by placing his cap in a hatbox after each game. (He discards caps that develop a curve.) Whenever Sherrill saves a game, his teammates—including Roberts—flip up their brims in tribute. Sherrill says his style is not a fashion statement but rather a sensitive reaction: "Because I'm left-handed, the bill of my cap would always bend a little bit lopsided, and other players would ride me because I couldn't get it quite right."

On the cutting edge: George Sherrill.

JOCK IN CHIEF CURLY LAMBEAU WRITES TO GERALD FORD

Gerald R. Ford, our 38th president, may not have been our finest chief executive, but he was probably the best athlete to live in the White House. He's certainly the only president to ever get a job offer from Curly Lambeau, the Green Bay Packers coach.

At the time, Ford was a University of Michigan senior, the departing captain of a Wolverine team that had won just one game in the 1934 season. But Ford had played so well and so hard at center and linebacker that he was invited to the East-West Shrine Game in San Francisco, which is where Lambeau saw him.

On stationery bearing the letterhead "Green Bay Football Corporation" and dated February 11, 1935, Lambeau wrote:

> Dear Ford:
>
> While on the Coast you told me you were undecided in regard to playing professional football.
>
> We plan on signing a center for the coming season and will pay you $110.00 per game if you wish to join the "Packers". Our league schedule is not drafted but we usually play fourteen games. We pay in full after each contest and all players are paid whether they play or not and, naturally, all injured players are paid immediately after each game.
>
> Will appreciate an early reply.
>
> With kindest personal regards, I am
>
> Sincerely,
>
> E. L. Curly Lambeau
>
> GREEN BAY FOOTBALL CORPORATION

> "There are no traffic jams along the extra mile."
> —Hall of Fame quarterback Roger Staubach

Ford turned down Lambeau's offer in order to accept a coaching position at Yale University and enroll in its law school. Who knows? If Lambeau had offered him, say, $125 a game, the course of history might have changed.

OPPOSITE PAGE: *Gerald Ford, captain of the Michigan Wolverines, 1934.*

READY FOR PRIME TIME

How do you get from the driveway to the playground? How do you go from shooting hoops by yourself to getting into a pickup game? Before he joined the And1 tour, Aaron "A.O." Owen was a fixture on the courts at Philadelphia's Connie Mack Recreation Center. Says Owen, "Basketball's great because you can play alone and all you need is a ball. But at the playground, all that shooting and dribbling by yourself won't translate to the game. That's not enough to get you picked." Here are A.O.'s suggestions on how to get off the fence and onto the court:

Don't travel. "Stick with the park that's closest. You know the skill level of the guys in your neighborhood, so you know if you'll be able to play. Also, the playground is like the club: You're more likely to get in if you know somebody."

Bring a buddy. "A lot of times you'll shoot to see who's captain, who does the picking. If you or your friend can shoot, the other one is guaranteed a spot."

Avoid rush hour. "At Connie Mack on Saturday and Sunday afternoons, it was all older guys, and there'd be 50 or so people waiting for a game. You could wait all day and never play."

Specialize. "Find one thing to be skilled at and work that. If you can rebound, if you're a shooter, if you're a dunker—do that while people are picking. Show that you can round out their team."

Swallow your inner whistle. "Some parks are rougher than others, so you have to show that hard fouls don't bother you. Play hard anyway, and they'll stop trying to take you out."

Don't tell a book by its cover. "There was this guy at a court in Newport Beach, California, wore slip-on Vans, a fisherman's hat, and cargo shorts. Looking at him, I didn't know if he was homeless or what. He ended up being one of the best players I've ever played against."

NBA star Allan Houston talks to the crowd at legendary Rucker Park in New York during the 5th Annual Father Knows Best Celebrity 2-on-2 Basketball Game on June 14, 2008.

GOLDEN PARACHUTES
SPORTS KICKED OUT OF THE OLYMPICS

Baseball and softball will not be included in the 2012 Olympics in London. But at least they're in good, bad, and weird company. These are the other sports that have been kicked out of the games:

The worst round in the history of golf's U.S. Open belongs to J. D. Tucker, who shot a 157 in the first round of the 1898 Open at the Myopia Hunt Club in South Hamilton, Massachusetts. The next day he pared 57 strokes off his score for an even 100.

Sport	Last Appearance in Olympics
Cricket	1900
Croquet	1900
Basque pelota	1900
Golf	1904
Roque	1904
Lacrosse	1908
Jeu de paume	1908
Rackets	1908
Motorboating	1908
Tug-of-war	1920
Rugby	1924
Polo	1936

The tug-of-war event during the 1920 Olympic Games in Antwerp, Belgium.

THE MASTER A GOLF LESSON FROM BOBBY JONES

The essence of golf is integrity, in no small part because one of its greatest players, Bobby Jones, was also one of its most honorable. A true renaissance man who studied engineering at Georgia Tech, English literature at Harvard, and law at Emory, Jones won 13 major tournaments between 1923 and his retirement from competition, in 1930. He then co-designed Augusta National and helped found the Masters.

He might have had one more major, the U.S. Open in 1925, had he not been so honest. During the final playoff, at the Worcester Country Club, Jones hit his ball into the long grass on the steep bank of the 11th green. As he addressed the ball, he thought he saw it move. He turned to the marshals and called a two-stroke penalty on himself. The marshals conferred and questioned members of the gallery to see whether anyone else had seen the ball move. Nobody had, so the marshals left the call up to Jones, who insisted that the penalty be assessed. He lost the Open by a single stroke.

When praised for his honesty, Jones replied, "You might as well praise me for not breaking into banks. There is only one way to play this game."

No wonder the annual USGA sportsmanship award is named for Bobby Jones.

Bobby Jones on his way to victory during the British Open Championship at St Andrews, 1927.

> **The 10th hole at the Old Course in St. Andrews, Scotland, is named for Bobby Jones, who withdrew in frustration during the third round of the 1921 British Open while on the 11th hole.**

"BOOM GOES THE DYNAMITE"
A SPORTSCAST FOR THE AGES

It's widely acknowledged as the worst sports broadcast ever, 3 minutes and 54 seconds of unintended comedic cringe that has earned a permanent place on YouTube (http://www.youtube.com/watch?v=W45DRy7M1no).

The time. March 2005.

The place. The Ball State University television studio.

The circumstance. The scheduled anchor for the *NewsLink @ Nine* sportscast had canceled.

The hapless volunteer replacement. Brian Collins, a 19-year-old telecommunications freshman from Milan, Ohio.

Brian figured, How hard can it be, reading some scores, breezing through the highlights? Unfortunately, the person on the teleprompter was also new and accidentally fast-forwarded through the script. So Brian could only pick out a word here or there before the copy disappeared from the prompter screen.

> "Not only is there more to life than basketball, there's a lot more to basketball than basketball."
> —NBA coach Phil Jackson

Now, he did have the typewritten script in front of him, in case of emergency. Alas, the pages were hopelessly out of order. So nothing Brian said matched up to what was being shown. He kept looking at the wrong TV monitor. Somebody walked behind him during the telecast. At one point during the torturous broadcast, Brian glanced at someone off camera and mouthed the words "I'm so sorry."

Whereas a lesser man might have walked off the set, Brian sighed and soldiered on. When he got to the Nets-Pacers highlights, he was winging it: *"Later he gets the rebound . . . passes it to the man . . . shoots it . . . and boom goes the dynamite."*

The broadcast became legend, in part because Ball State alumnus David Letterman got wind of it and invited Brian to appear on the *Late Show*. ESPN anchor Scott Van Pelt sent Brian a note of encouragement and still uses "boom goes the dynamite" as a shoutout. As for Brian, not only did he survive the experience, but he now works for KXXV-TV in Waco, Texas—as a news reporter.

> **"Sports do not build character. They reveal it."**
> —John Wooden

Four of the top 10 scorers for the 1976–77 NBA season were refugees from the American Basketball Association: Billy Knight, David Thompson, Dan Issel, and George Gervin.

THE HEATER
CHRIS YOUNG ON HOW TO THROW IT BY THEM

It goes by many names: heater, hummer, cheese, cheddar, smoke, steam, dart, dead red, hard one, number one, bullet, blazer, bee at the knee, gas, pumper, aspirin tablet, and—in scoutspeak—little baseball. As in "he throws little baseballs."

We're speaking, of course, of the fastball, and it is an essential tool of the baseball or softball pitcher. Whether you throw as hard as Nolan Ryan did (95–100 mph) or as soft as Jamie Moyer (80–85 mph), you need to have a fastball to get an out or at least to set up the pitches that will get the outs.

For tips on the baseball side, we went to one of the younger students of the game, San Diego Padres right-hander Chris Young, who also happens to be a graduate of Princeton University with a major in political science. Granted, at 6 foot 10, Young is probably taller than you, but he also possesses what coaches call an educated hand, meaning that he has the ability to alter his grips and make the ball respond. We'll let him explain the two basic types of fastballs: the four-seamer, which is his bread-and-butter pitch, and the two-seamer, also known as a sinker:

The four-seam fastball is a control pitch, a pitch that has less movement than a sinker, slider, curveball, changeup, or knuckleball. Although it is a control pitch, it can also be a power pitch that can have the illusion of rising when thrown up in the zone. Nolan Ryan is the best example of a power pitcher who often used a high four-seam fastball to finish hitters off.

The beauty of the four-seam fastball is the simplicity of it. You simply grip the baseball across the seam's horseshoe with your index and middle fingers, thumb directly underneath the ball. Your index and middle fingers are therefore touching the seams of the baseball in four places. You do not manipulate the pitch; just throw the baseball normally, with your hand and forearm forming a 90-degree angle at the wrist as you reach the release point.

As you release the ball, your hand comes through with a powerful downward flick from the wrist. This allows you to stay behind the ball, creating a perfect back-spin on the ball when it is released, causing the rising effect when thrown properly. In my biased opinion, there is no better feeling than reaching back and throwing a hard four-seam fastball right by a batter. It's my best pitch, but ironically most hitters would like to think it's their best pitch to hit.

The two-seam fastball is a pitch that uses movement to get a hitter to put less than a perfect swing on it. The speed of the pitch combined with the movement of the ball makes it difficult for a hitter to hit the ball on the barrel of the bat. Unlike a four-seam fastball, there are many variations on how to grip a two-seam fastball.

The most common way is to place the index and middle fingers just inside or along the narrow part of the seams, usually where the trademark of the ball is, thumb underneath the ball. Neither finger should be across the seams, but rather they should be running with the seams. You then throw the two-seam fastball the same way as a four-seam fastball, letting the grip cause the movement. A properly thrown two-seam fastball by a right-handed pitcher will sink or run down and into a right-handed hitter, and a two-seamer by a left-handed pitcher will sink or run down and into a left-handed hitter.

To create greater movement, some pitchers offset their thumb underneath their index finger, causing them to stay inside the ball and creating even more movement. Spending the 2007 season with future Hall-of-Famer Greg Maddux taught me that working with various types of fastballs is a never-ending game of trial and error. We pitchers are always tinkering on off days, searching for any little grip change that might make the ball dance and dart even more the next time we take the mound.

Broadcast legends Tim McCarver and Brent Musburger first met in 1959, when McCarver was a catcher for Keokuk and Musburger was an umpire in the Class A Midwest League.

THE CHANGEUP TODD JONES ON HOW TO FOOL THEM

A few years ago, **Dr. Joseph Chandler,** an orthopedic consultant for the Atlanta Braves, asked more than 100 pitchers in the Braves' organization for a recommended age for throwing a curveball. Most of them said not before 15. Yet if you watch the Little League World Series, the annual international baseball tournament for kids ages 10 to 12, you'll see pitchers throw curveballs at an alarming rate: 40 to 60 percent of their total pitches. The short-term effect is lots of strikeouts. The long-term effect is permanent damage to elbows that are not mature enough to withstand the strain.

A safer and often more effective off-speed pitch is the changeup. Longtime major league reliever Todd Jones is one of its champions:

If I had to teach a 10-year-old how to throw a change, I'd tell him to grip the baseball like he's throwing a fastball but split his index and middle fingers a little on each side of the ball. Then I'd tell him to throw that pitch as hard as he can.

The idea is for the unconventional grip to take the speed off the pitch. If that grip doesn't work, move on to another grip and ask your catcher how the pitch looks coming out of your hand. You have to sell the changeup to the hitter. He has to believe a fastball is coming. If a pitcher slows his arm down, the pitch has no deception and becomes nothing more than batting practice.

The grip is everything, but there's no one way to do it. You can also choke the ball back in your hand toward your palm. Or you can use your middle and ring fingers to apply pressure on the seams, rather than the index and middle fingers. That's what many people call the circle change, because you make a circle with your index finger and thumb and let the ball come off the middle and ring digits.

Granted, the changeup doesn't have the machismo of the fastball or the dramatic break of the curveball or the slider. Heck, it doesn't even have a nickname beyond change of pace or change. But it does have pitchers like Jones, Trevor Hoffman, John Smoltz, and Johan Santana on its side.

The first official Little Leaguer to play major league baseball was pitcher Joey Jay, who made his debut with the Milwaukee Braves in 1953.

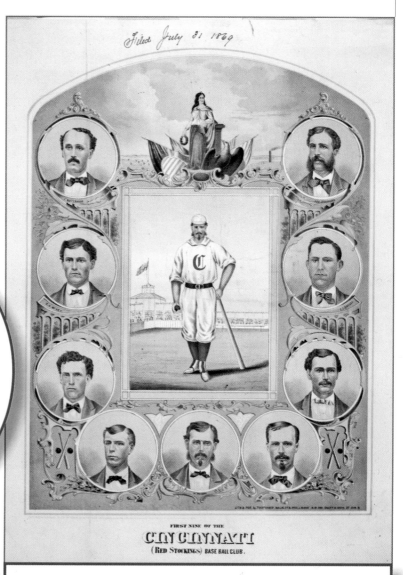

Baseball's first full-time strength and conditioning coach was Otis Douglas, a former NFL player who helped the 1961 Cincinnati Reds win the National League pennant.

PRIVATE QUARTERS INSIDE DONOVAN McNABB'S LOCKER

Have you ever wondered what the locker of an NFL quarterback looks like? Well, we have, and Donovan McNabb of the Philadelphia Eagles was kind enough to show us around his locker area at Lincoln Financial Field. Pull up a chair, because it has a lot more than you might think:

When you start out, there's not that much stuff in your locker. Then you get more and more shirts. . . . I have stuff the Eagles don't want anymore, Christmas items. We moved over from the Vet—not that much room in your locker there. Over here, there's a bit more space. I have a lot of exciting things in here.

Let's start at the bottom. My Nike shoes are here. Up until two years ago, those shoes were Reeboks. Now I'm with Nike. So I have about 12 or 15 pairs of their shoes here.

Then we have my brand of protein shakes. Two exciting flavors, vanilla cream and cookies 'n' cream, because those are the flavors I got for free. Free is me; I love free. I drink these usually twice a day. Neuropath drink mix sends messages to the brain waves and vitamins into the system. I mix that into protein shakes once a day.

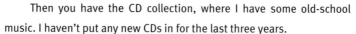

Then you have the CD collection, where I have some old-school music. I haven't put any new CDs in for the last three years.

"I have my Billy Blanks Tae Bo workout tapes. They're my secret weapon to prepare myself for the season. A little different workout—running, lifting, lots of Tae Bo exercises and instruction. I do these at home or back in the back room, where we have a quiet area with a small 13-inch screen. [*Laughs.*] Billy looks small.

In the next cubby, you have your body soap. I prefer the milk-and-honey and cucumber-melon scents to bring out the smells. You don't want to smell funky coming in or leaving practice. Lotion is key—cocoa butter keeps the skin nice and soft. They give you soap here, but this way you have a little flavor, a little something different than anyone else.

Moving over to the shelf, I have my Bible. Next to it, my Syracuse hat and helmet because we definitely need the prayers to go out to Syracuse University. [*Laughs.*] For Bibles, I have the NIV and the King James Version. We have Bible study here once a week.

Next to the Bible, I have Tony Dungy's book *Quiet Strength*. He's done so much in his career, and, obviously, going through what he went through with his family and to be able to tell the world about it—it's a great book. Number one on the bestseller list for a while, I think. I was fortunate enough to get it. The other books are a Johnny U bio and *Noah's Rainbow* by Dave Fleming.

I have a couple hats up there on the shelf. Some free Planters peanuts. Whatever's free, I have it. My Syracuse football. As you know, I went there, so I'm showing the love for my university around here. Shirt collection—Syracuse shirt, "Real Men Are Orange." It was the Orangemen when I was there, but now they're just the Orange. I have a shirt from the Rock, Dwayne Johnson—he sent a shirt to one of our strength-and-conditioning coaches and one to me. I got that four, five years ago, but he's a great guy and I still wear it. I haven't met him personally, but I thought that was cool.

The artwork was a gift sent to me in 2004. Someone made that when they wanted an autograph, and I like the picture. It looks like me mixed with a little bit of Dhani Jones. I thought it was creative, so I've kept it up there for a while. Definitely cool and different.

This is a letter sent to me by a fan, Ms. Pena. She was saying I inspired her and told me to keep on fighting. This was from 2004, when we had a great year. I've had it up there ever since. The other letter is from one of my former coaches, Leslie Frazier, now the D coordinator at Minnesota. It has some scriptures written on it.

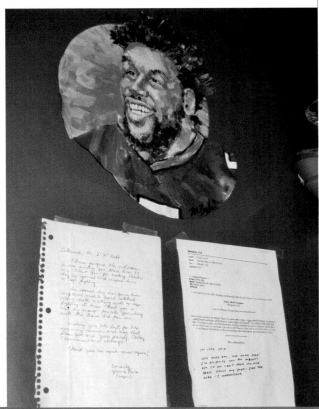

I keep important things in my locker that mean a lot to me. But there's also some stuff that I probably don't need that has been here for years. I have this puzzle given to me by an old team-mate of mine, Chad Lewis, who went over to Asia. I can't do it right at all, but I keep it over here.

I have a lot of different types of pictures. This is the award I got with Harry Kalas, voice of the Phillies, and this is me with the Wanamaker Award. Here's me and Tim Couch, number one and number two picks of the 1999 draft, working out on the field together. This is a picture and flag from the Marine Corps—we have some troops come out to practice during training camp, and we get a chance to thank them for what they do for us.

Up here, I have a flat-screen TV. When I'm in my locker sometimes, I throw something on so I can watch. Almost everyone can see it; there's TVs everywhere, but not many guys can say they have a TV in their locker.

Tour over, McNabb was asked what three items he would take home from the locker. "My body-face soap and lotion—that's one. My Bible. And my mother always said to have clean underwear, so I'd take that, too."

"The alumni wanted a big-name coach. They got a long-name coach."

—longtime Syracuse football coach Ben Schwartzwalder, upon being hired in 1949

TRUE CALLING

HOW MANY CY YOUNGS WOULD CY YOUNG HAVE WON?

Denton True Young won 511 games in his 22 major league seasons (1890–1911), pitching 7,356 innings with an ERA of 2.63. So it's quite fitting that an award was named after him, given first, beginning in 1956, to the best pitcher in the majors and then, starting in 1967, to the best pitcher in his respective league.

But that raises the question, How many Cy Young Awards would the man also known as Cyclone have won? By employing modern-day standards and preferences to the context of Young's time, we can determine that he would have been a clear winner in 1892, when he pitched for Cleveland and led the National League in wins (36) and ERA (1.93); in 1901, when he won 33 for

Boston with an AL-leading 1.62 ERA; in 1902, when he won 32 games and threw 41 complete games for the Red Sox; and 1903, when he had 28 victories, an ERA of 2.08, and seven shutouts (that same season, over in the National League, Christy Mathewson had better numbers).

Young had other outstanding seasons but probably would have lost out to the Giants' Amos Rusie in 1893 (inferior ERA), to Baltimore's Chick Hoffer in 1895 (inferior team), to Kid Nichols in 1896 and 1898 (inferior stats), and to Jay Hughes in 1899 (inferior winning percentage *and* team).

So there you have it: Cy Young would probably have won his own award four times. Or three fewer times than Roger Clemens.

Cy Young warms up for the
Cleveland Naps, circa 1910.

SIGH YOUNG THE WRONG DELIVERY FOR A PITCHER

The Cy Young Award itself is an extraordinarily heavy plaque on which a silver hand holding a baseball rises up out of a baseball diamond. It's weird enough to carry a curse—and it does. Ask Vern Law, Randy Jones, Sparky Lyle, Steve Stone, Pete Vuckovich, John Denny, LaMarr Hoyt, Mark Davis, Doug Drabek, Jack McDowell, Pat Hentgen, Eric Gagne, and Barry Zito, all of whom flamed out shortly after winning the award. Denny McLain lost both his awards in a house fire. And we know what happened to the Rocket after he won his seven.

Steve Stone, who went from 25-7 to 4-7 after winning the award in 1980, tells this story: "The day the crate arrived was going to be the greatest day of my life. I mean, this was the Cy Young Award, the culmination of all the pain and blood and sweat and tears. But when I opened the box, I pulled out the plaque and saw that they had sent me Steve Carlton's Cy Young Award."

"Awards become corroded. Friends gather no dust."
—Jesse Owens

SEVEN WONDERS
YOU HAVE TO BE THERE TO APPRECIATE THEM

If you've got a little time—and money—on your hands, and you want a global view of athletics, may we suggest visiting these Seven Wonders of the Sports World, each in a different region of the world:

Asia: National Swimming Center, Beijing, China. Completed in 2006, the so-called Water Cube has such innovations as a Teflon-like panel exterior that allows the sun to heat the pools, a system for collecting and using rainwater, and a steel-frame undergirding that mimics the structural properties of soap bubbles and can withstand nearly any seismic occurrence. The Cube was apparently built to accommodate the unprecedented performance by swimmer Michael Phelps, who won eight gold medals in the Cube at the 2008 Summer Olympics.

Oceania: Melbourne Cricket Ground, Melbourne, Australia. Built in 1853, the MCG is Australia's largest stadium and one of the world's premier cricket grounds. In the past, more than 120,000 people have crammed into the stadium for major events, but renovations and safety regulations now keep the capacity closer to 100,000 (98,000 seated, 2,000 standing). The stadium is known colloquially as the G and more soberly as the spiritual home of Australian sport.

Middle East: Ski Dubai, Dubai, United Arab Emirates. Located in the sun-baked desert emirate, this 242,000-square-foot indoor ski resort boasts five downhill ski runs varying in difficulty (the longest is 1,312 feet with a 197-foot fall), a cross-country trail, a 295-foot quarter pipe for snowboarders, a chair lift, and the world's largest indoor snow park (with tobogganing hills, a twin-track bobsled ride, a snowball-throwing gallery, and a snow cavern). While the outside temperature ranges from 50 to 118 degrees Fahrenheit, the ski area remains at 28 degrees, with 2 feet of snowpack beneath a layer of powder laid down fresh each night.

South America: Estádio do Maracaña, Rio de Janeiro, Brazil. The home field of the legendary Pelé, Estádio do Maracaña was built to host the 1950 World Cup finals. Its official capacity is 180,000, although a reported 220,000—the biggest-ever crowd for a football match—were on hand for the decisive game between Brazil and Uruguay. The mountain backdrop beyond the bowl's rim reinforces the spectacular atmosphere.

North America: Indianapolis Motor Speedway, Speedway, Indiana, United States. For sheer magnitude, nothing tops the Brickyard. It can host up to 250,000 spectators, easily making it the world's largest sports venue. (Infield seating raises that figure to 400,000.) Built in 1909, it has expanded over time from its original 320 acres to 559. The 2½-mile oval was designated a National Historic Landmark in 1987. If there's no race, you can always play the nine-hole golf course in the infield.

Africa: Rift Valley Province, Kenya. This lush region has given rise to the impoverished African nation's domination of distance running. World-class marathoners like Kip Keino, Mike Boit, and Moses Tanui made themselves into champions with a punishing regimen of training runs that saw them cover up to 175 miles in a week at elevations as high as 10,000 feet above sea level. Talk about a breathtaking experience.

Europe: Wembley Stadium, London, England. The 90,000-seat stadium, expected to be the centerpiece of the 2012 Summer Olympics, has undergone a significant renovation in preparation for the games. The signature 98.3-foot twin towers of the original Wembley have been replaced by a dramatic 436-foot arch, which will support 5,000 tons of the 7,000-ton movable roof. This design eliminates the need for pillars, which could obscure visitors' views. The arch—visible throughout London—is the longest single-span roof structure in the world.

THE ROPES

For most boxers, the workout begins with a length of rope. Skipping rope, or jumping rope, is a time-honored tradition in the fight game for a reason: There is no better way to get the blood flowing, the feet working, the hands moving, the joints jumping. And there may be no better man to teach you the ropes than Sugar Shane Mosley, a former lightweight, welterweight, and junior-middleweight champion known for his rope dexterity.

The proper size, around 8 feet long, can be measured like this: Drop the rope to the floor, step on the midpoint with one foot, and pick up the handles—they should come up to your waist.

I like to use a light rope, plastic, not a weighted one, so the rope moves fast. Some guys like a heavier rope to strengthen their forearms and grip, but I want the cardio aspect of it. I want to get into a rhythm, listen to the rope hit the ground, listen to the sound of the wind. It helps your rhythm.

So does music. Anything with a beat, but I listen to Lil Wayne a lot.

I typically do 10 to 15 minutes to start my workout, and I might finish with some more. I've been skipping rope since I was six, at Roosevelt Elementary in Pomona. We had a thing every year where we skipped rope to be healthy, and I'd see the girls doing double Dutch and stuff, and I wanted to copy that. I've also watched films of Roberto Duran and Sugar Ray Robinson.

Other things to remember: The width of your feet should be a little less than your shoulders. Don't jump too high. Land on the balls of your feet, not on your heels. Flick your wrists counterclockwise, let the rope skip on the floor under your feet, and repeat. Use your wrists only to increase your revolutions, to pick up speed and increase your heart rate.

As you get more adept with the rope, you might be able to pull off crisscrosses, doubles, and triples. Mosley sometimes flicks his wrists clockwise to freshen things up, and you'll often see him do the alternate foot jump to double the number of skips.

In a gym, you can usually tell the novice boxer by the way he jumps rope. But Mosley doesn't see a correlation between skipping and fighting. "Boxing is a mental game," he says, "so even if you aren't good with the rope, that doesn't mean you can't fight."

Sugar Ray Robinson gets the jump in 1951.

The Elias Sports Bureau is the repository for statistics involving the major team sports, so a lot of information passes through its offices, in New York City. We asked Steve Hirdt, the executive vice president of Elias, for a few stumpers that might surprise even knowledgeable sports fans or win you a bet. Here are five (with the answers below):

1. Giants Stadium has been the site of more NFL regular-season games than any other building. Which facility comes in second?
2. Which player, certain to be inducted into the Hall of Fame, was on the receiving end of Brett Favre's first NFL completion in 1992?
3. In recent years, Ichiro Suzuki, Hideki Matsui, and Kosuke Fukudome have started All-Star Games in center field in their first season in the majors. Prior to those three players, who was the only rookie to start an All-Star Game in center field?
4. Multiple choice: In 62 seasons, how many times has the team that led the NBA in regular-season free-throw percentage gone on to win the NBA championship that season? (a) 1; (b) 5; (c) 10; (d) 16; (e) 24
5. Which Hall of Famer hit the most home runs at Yankee Stadium as a visiting player?

Answers: 1. Wrigley Field in Chicago; 2. Brett Favre, following a deflection; 3. Richie Ashburn of the Phillies, in 1948; 4. (a) 1: the Minneapolis Lakers in 1953–54; 5. Goose Goslin: 32 home runs (from 1921 to 1938)

> **"If you're lucky enough to find a guy with a lot of head and a lot of heart, he's never going to come off the field second."**
> —Vince Lombardi

Chicago Bear Gale Sayers (number 40) runs through the Washington Redskins defense at Wrigley Field on September 15, 1968.

UNCOMMON SCENTS DON'T STOP TO SMELL THE HOCKEY BAGS

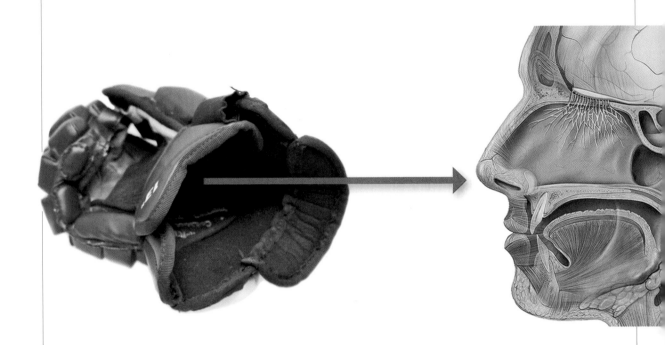

The smell of success is not always sweet. In fact, the aromas of locker rooms and equipment bags and team buses can take some getting used to. Along with the stench comes a more serious issue: bacteria. Methicillin-resistant *Staphylococcus aureus* (MRSA), a highly contagious mutation of the common staph infection, thrives in soiled pads and equipment and is hitting athletes with alarming frequency. Where there's stink, there's health risk.

And no sport has quite the pungency of ice hockey, with its combination of wet, sweat, and gear; the gloves alone would offend a skunk. So we asked an expert on the subject, New York Rangers equipment manager Acacio Marques, for some tips on how to get rid of the reek and protect players from potentially fatal infections.

"The key is to get everything dry," says Marques.

If it stays wet, bacteria tends to grow a lot quicker. We hang our gear up every night. Most youth-hockey players don't do that. It probably stays in their bag wet, and that's why it starts to stink. Rookies come in here from juniors or from Europe, and you can tell that their stuff has never been hung. It smells like puke.

There's a drying room at our practice rink. After road trips, we go there, hang the gear, and crank the heat. It gets to about 100 degrees. The next morning everything is dry. Believe it or not, that really helps.

We also use a Sani Sport machine that disinfects with bactericide and ozone gas. And we put an MRSA-killing additive in the washing machine with towels and underwear. We've never had a guy get a staph infection, and we want to keep it that way.

Although you may not have the resources the Rangers have, you can follow their example by drying out wet equipment after each practice. And there are plenty of everyday disinfectant cleaners and sprays you can buy to kill germs. Hockey also has a cottage industry of products designed to take the PU out of equipment.

But as Marques admits, the sport will never smell like roses. "A 10-year-old pair of skates that a guy wears barefoot is always going to stink a little."

The shortest player in NHL history was 5-foot-3 goalie Roy "Shrimp" Worters, who played in 484 games between 1925 and 1937.

REEL BAD

Speaking of stink, here is Jeffrey Lyons's list of the five worst sports movies of all time, again with trailers:

> Abebe Bikila of Ethiopia won the marathon gold at the 1960 Rome Olympics while running barefoot and the 1964 Tokyo gold while competing 40 days after an appendectomy.

Personal Best (1982, track and field). "The only ass you need to whip is your own."
—Kenny Moore as swimmer Denny Stites to Mariel Hemingway as runner Chris Cahill

The Fish That Saved Pittsburgh (1979, basketball). "The astrology thing is just a mirror for us to look into. Our magic is made of sweat, strain, and pride. Now that's what I'm taking back out on the damn court."
—Julius Erving as Moses Guthrie

Wimbledon (2004, tennis). "Listen, you may have read about Lizzie Bradbury and myself being . . . involved, so to speak, . . . but I'd like to take this opportunity to set the record straight. I read the papers this morning, and they seemed to imply that Lizzie had let me down in some way. That's just not the case. The truth is I let her down. I let her down, and for that I will always be truly sorry. Listen, I'm not in the habit of pouring my heart out on television or pouring my heart out at all. . . . Forgive me. Lizzie Bradbury . . . Lizzie is the reason that I'm here today. That's all I really came here to say, so thank you."
—Paul Bettany as tennis pro Peter Colt, to tennis commentator Mary Carillo as herself

> **"I give 'em the hip, then I take it away."**
> —Jim Thorpe

Sylvester Stallone in
Over the Top, *1987.*

Rocky V (1990, boxing). "I'm officially expired."
>   —Sylvester Stallone as Rocky Balboa, to the promoter trying to get him
>   back in the ring

Over the Top (1987, arm wrestling). "The world meets nobody half-way. When you want something, you gotta take it."
>   —Sylvester Stallone as trucker and arm wrestler Lincoln Hawk

> **Tennis balls are fuzzy because their sixteenth-century ancestors were made with the hair of Scotland's enemies.**

BEND IT LIKE KLJESTAN

Sacha Kljestan is a rising star on the U.S. national soccer team and a midfielder for Chivas USA, a team that shares a stadium, the Home Depot Center, with the Los Angeles Galaxy. That means Sacha and his Chivas teammates get dressed down the hall from David Beckham, a player famous for his ability to bend free kicks with an uncanny combination of power and accuracy. Kljestan, who is of Slovakian descent, has become one of the league's better free-kick takers, but he says he does not exactly bend it like Beckham. Here's his take:

Personally, I like to approach the ball at about a 45-degree angle, but Beckham, the master, approaches at closer to 90 degrees. It is all a matter of preference, and by far the most important thing of all is to practice.

When taking a free kick, so many factors come into play, especially when shooting from close range, when you need to be able to bend the ball over the wall (which is usually the tallest guys) and then get the ball to dip back down into the goal. The first thing you need to do is put everything else out of your mind and focus 100 percent on just this free kick. I try to visualize where I am going to put the ball and try to put it in a spot where the goalie can't get to it. Then I take a breath and hit the ball with the inside part of my foot and try to create enough spin to bend the ball over the wall.

You have to take thousands of free kicks in practice to the point where you feel you can put the ball exactly where you want it. It's very similar to a golfer working on one shot for hours, hoping that in his next round he'll get a chance to execute that very shot.

A very wise man and mentor of mine growing up always told me the same story about free kicks. He told me how he got to watch Chelsea train quite a few times, and every day after practice Gianfranco Zola would practice his free kicks, one after the other. One Friday he watched him in training practicing his free kicks, and the next day he had a free kick from exactly where he had been practicing his free kicks. Sure enough, Zola bent it over the wall and into the net. I think of that story every day after training, when I do my work.

Members of the Liberia national soccer team escaped imprisonment by holding Gambia to a goalless draw in 1980; the Liberian head of state, Master Sergeant Samuel Doe, had threatened to jail them if they lost.

SPORTUGUESE

WHAT'S A BLUTARSKY?
A QUIZ ON SPORTS LINGO

The language of sports—Sportuguese, if you will—has its mysteries. You may know that the expression "throwing the ball around the horn" is derived from the navigational feat of sailing around Cape Horn and that *gridiron* comes from the griddle that fields with hash marks resemble. But did you know that *Mendoza line* was coined by Royals third baseman George Brett to denote shortstop Mario Mendoza's typical average of .200? Or that in five of his nine seasons, Mendoza was actually below his eponymous demarcation?

Here's a little quiz in which we ask you to match 12 terms with their correct definition. If you get three right, you're above the Mendoza line:

The mashie niblick at bottom left was one of the clubs that Francis Ouimet used to win the 1913 U.S. Open

1. goofy
2. Blutarsky
3. corridor of uncertainty
4. keepie uppie
5. nutmeg
6. cherry-picking
7. butterfly
8. bolo
9. golden sombrero
10. bug boy
11. vigorish
12. mashie niblick

"It's not whether you win or lose—
but whether *I* win or lose."
—British golfer Sandy Lyle

A. the amount charged by a bookmaker for his or her services, in order to make sure the bookie makes money on a wager no matter what the outcome

B. a stance on a skateboard, surfboard, snowboard, or wakeboard in which the right foot is on the front of the board

C. the style of goaltending in which the goaltender covers the lower part of the net with his or her leg pads, leaving the upper portion of the net somewhat exposed

D. an obsolete golf club that roughly corresponds to a modern-day 7-, 8-, or 9-iron

E. a quarterback's zero passer rating for a game; also known as a Rex Grossman

F. a game of juggling a soccer ball using the feet, thighs, knees, chest, and head

G. a baseball player's striking out four times in one game

H. an apprentice jockey

I. a type of punch that's set up by swinging one arm in a circular motion, then hitting one's opponent with the other

J. the area in which a cricket ball can be pitched, usually a narrow line on and just outside a batsman's off stump

K. the act of hanging out in the offensive zone (thus not playing defense) and waiting for an offensive opportunity to arise without much effort

L. a play in which a soccer player kicks the ball through the defender's legs

Key: 1-B, 2-E, 3-J, 4-F, 5-L, 6-K, 7-C, 8-I, 9-G, 10-H, 11-A, 12-D

MIGHTY CASEY
THE MAN WHO WROTE AMERICA'S BEST-KNOWN POEM

"Casey at the Bat" begins "The Outlook wasn't brilliant for the Mudville nine that day" and ends with . . . Well, you know. What you might not know is that it was a one-hit wonder written by a man, Ernest Lawrence Thayer, who spent many of his 77 years looking after his family's textile mill in Worcester, Massachusetts. But Thayer had studied at Harvard and worked at the *Lampoon* alongside William Randolph Hearst. So when Hearst's father gave his son the San Francisco *Examiner* to run in 1885, the young man brought along Thayer and two other *Lampoon* writers. On June 3, 1888, *The Examiner* published "Casey at the Bat," which Thayer—under his pen name, Phin—had written with Boston baseball star Mike "King" Kelly in mind. There was no immediate response to the poem.

It was republished a few weeks later, however, in the New York *Sun* and brought to the attention of the legendary actor DeWolf Hopper, who was performing at the Wallack Theatre before an audience that included members of the New York and visiting Chicago baseball teams. The date of the performance was August 14, 1888, which happened to be Thayer's 25th birthday.

Thanks to Hopper, "Casey" soon became the most famous poem in the land. As the game's patriarch, Albert Spalding, once wrote, "Love has its sonnets galore. War has its epics in heroic verse. Tragedy its

CASEY AT THE BAT

By
PHINEAS THAYER

Illustrations by
DAN SAYRE GROESBECK

CHICAGO
A. C. McCLURG & CO.
1912

KELLY,
(C.Boston.)

OLD JUDGE & GYPSY QUEEN CIGARETTES

> **Hank Gowdy, a catcher and first baseman for the New York Giants and Boston Braves from 1910 to 1930, is the only major leaguer to have seen combat in both world wars.**

somber story in measured lines. Baseball has 'Casey at the Bat.'" Thayer, however, lived in relative obscurity. He did recite "Casey" at a Harvard class reunion in 1895, but he must not have been very good. Hopper himself once said, "I have heard many others give 'Casey.' Fond mamas have brought their sons to me to hear their childish voices lisp the poem. But Thayer's was the worst of all."

Read more than 100 years later, though, it holds up rather well. Because of "Casey," somewhere hearts are light.

King Kelly, the supposed inspiration for Casey.

FROM THE PEN
A POEM BY THE LATE DAN QUISENBERRY

I f "Casey at the Bat" is the best poem about an athlete, what's the best poem *by* an athlete? Here's a candidate, written by Dan Quisenberry, the submarining reliever who saved 244 games and entertained countless teammates and writers during his 12-year career. He penned "Baseball Cards" before he died, of brain cancer, at the age of 45, in 1988. This can be found in *On Days Like This* (Helicon Nine), a collection of his poems:

BASEBALL CARDS

that first baseball card I saw myself
in a triage of rookies
atop the bodies
that made the hill
we played king of
I am the older one
the one on the right
game-face sincere
long red hair unkempt
a symbol of the '70s
somehow a sign of manhood
you don't see
how my knees shook on my debut
or my desperation to make it

the second one I look boyish with a
    gap-toothed smile
the smile of a guy who has it his way
expects it
I rode the wave's crest
of pennant and trophies
I sat relaxed with one thought
"I can do this"
you don't see
me stay up till two
reining in nerves
or post-game hands that shook involuntarily

glory years catch action shots
arm whips and body contortions
a human catapult the backs of those cards
cite numbers
that tell stories of saves, wins, flags, records

handshakes, butt slaps, celebration mobs
you can't see
the cost of winning
lines on my forehead under the hat
trench line between my eyes
you don't see my wife, daughter and son
left behind

the last few cards
I do not smile
I grim-face the camera
tight lipped
no more forced poses to win fans
eyes squint
scanning distance
crow's-feet turn into eagle's claws
you don't see
the quiver in my heart
knowledge that it is over
just playing out the end

I look back
at who I thought I was
or used to be
now, trying to be funny
I tell folks
I used to be famous
I used to be good
they say
we thought you were bigger
I say
I was

Baseball pioneer Albert G. Spalding once wrote, "Modern baseball had been born in the brain of an American soldier. It received its baptism in the bloody days of our Nation's direst danger. It had its earliest evolution when soldiers, North and South, were striving to forget their foes by cultivating, through this grand game, fraternal friendship with comrades in arms."

Spalding's words are given special meaning in this 1863 lithograph of Union prisoners playing baseball under Confederate guard in a prison in Salisbury, North Carolina.

MIGHTIEST FEAT (OLYMPICS)
THE DAY BOB BEAMON DID THE IMPOSSIBLE

A year before Neil Armstrong took his small step for a man, Bob Beamon made a giant leap that was almost as fantastic as a walk on the moon. It was in the long jump at the 1968 Summer Olympics in Mexico City, and it's still hard to fathom.

Beamon, a 22-year-old from Jamaica, Queens, had recently been suspended by the University of Texas, El Paso, for refusing to compete against Brigham Young University because of its racist policies. But after agreeing to be trained by Olympic long jumper Ralph Boston, he was the clear favorite in the event. Still, he almost didn't make the finals, qualifying on his third try after fouling on his first two attempts.

Beamon described the moments before he sprinted down the track and leaped into history this way: "I felt that day very calm, very peaceful. When I stood there, I didn't hear anybody. I was very focused. When I jumped, there was nothing . . . but quietness."

The judges were initially unable to determine Beamon's distance because he had jumped beyond the range of the electronic monitor that performed that function. Measuring by hand, officials announced that Beamon had flown a mind-boggling 29 feet, 2.5 inches—nearly 2 feet farther than the previous record. The jump marked the first time anyone had jumped 29 feet. Heck, it marked the first time anyone had jumped 28 feet! When Boston told him the distance, Beamon collapsed to his knees and held his hands over his face in shock.

Although it was said that Beamon benefited that day from both Mexico City's high altitude and a strong trailing wind, scientific research later determined that those factors could not fully explain his achievement. Beamon himself never jumped beyond 27 feet again in his career. His record stood until 1991, when it was broken by Mike Powell's jump of 29 feet, 4.375 inches. But his Olympic record endures, as do the words of the defending Olympic champion, Britain's Lynn Davies, who told Beamon that day, "You have destroyed this event."

> **Hugo Friend, who won a bronze medal in the long jump at the 1906 Athens Olympics, later became the judge who presided over the 1921 trial in which members of the Black Sox were charged with throwing the 1919 World Series.**

OPPOSITE PAGE:

Bob Beamon breaks the world record in Mexico City.

SUPER STARS

At the very first Super Bowl, on January 15, 1967, at the Los Angeles Coliseum, the halftime entertainment was provided by the University of Michigan and University of Arizona marching bands. Since then, the halftime show has gotten bigger, sometimes better, and sometimes weirder. There's Super Bowl XXVII, when Michael Jackson performed at the Rose Bowl with 3,500 children, and Super Bowl XXXVIII, when his sister Janet Jackson had her "wardrobe malfunction" in Houston. And remember XXIX, when an actor playing Indiana Jones tried to capture the Lombardi Trophy? But for the truly bizarre, consider this: Carol Channing has performed in two more Super Bowls than the Detroit Lions.

Here's a recap of the halftime acts, numeral by numeral:

I	University of Arizona and University of Michigan bands
II	Grambling State University band
III	Florida A&M University band
IV	Carol Channing
V	Florida A&M University band
VI	Ella Fitzgerald; Carol Channing; Al Hirt; U.S. Marine Corps Drill Team
VII	University of Michigan band; Woody Herman
VIII	University of Texas band; fiddler Judy Mallett (Miss Texas, 1973)
IX	Mercer Ellington's band; Grambling State University band
X	Up with People
XI	Los Angeles Unified All-City Band
XII	Tyler Junior College Apache Belles; Al Hirt; Pete Fountain
XIII	Ken Hamilton; various Caribbean bands
XIV	Up with People
XV	Southern University band; Helen O'Connell
XVI	Up with People
XVII	Los Angeles Super Drill Team
XVIII	University of Florida and Florida State University bands
XIX	Tops in Blue (members of the U.S. Air Force)
XX	Up with People
XXI	Southern California high school performers
XXII	Chubby Checker; the Rockettes; 88 grand pianos

The only reception tight end Percy Howard ever made in the NFL was a 34-yard touchdown pass from Cowboys QB Roger Staubach in Super Bowl X.

XXIII	Elvis Presto (The King impersonator)
XXIV	Pete Fountain; Doug Kershaw; Irma Thomas
XXV	New Kids on the Block
XXVI	Gloria Estefan; figure skaters Brian Boitano and Dorothy Hamill
XXVII	Michael Jackson and 3,500 children
XXVIII	Clint Black; Tanya Tucker; Travis Tritt; the Judds
XXIX	Indiana Jones impersonator; Patti LaBelle; Tony Bennett; Arturo Sandoval; the Miami Sound Machine
XXX	Diana Ross
XXXI	Blues Brothers (Dan Aykroyd, John Goodman, and James Belushi); ZZ Top; James Brown
XXXII	Boyz II Men; Smokey Robinson; Martha Reeves; the Temptations; Queen Latifah
XXXIII	Stevie Wonder; Gloria Estefan; Big Bad Voodoo Daddy; Savion Glover
XXXIV	Phil Collins; Christina Aguilera; Enrique Iglesias; Toni Braxton
XXXV	Aerosmith; 'N Sync; Britney Spears; Mary J. Blige; Nelly
XXXVI	U2

XXXVII	Shania Twain; No Doubt; Sting
XXXVIII	Jessica Simpson; Janet Jackson; Justin Timberlake; Nelly; P. Diddy; Kid Rock
XXXIX	Paul McCartney
XL	The Rolling Stones
XLI	Prince
XLII	Tom Petty and the Heartbreakers
XLIII	Bruce Springsteen and the E Street Band

Unless you can hit your first serve in every time (70 percent of the time is considered good), you need a second serve. So we asked Robert Lansdorp, the man who coached Tracy Austin, Pete Sampras, Lindsay Davenport, and Maria Sharapova to the top, for some advice on plan B. Here's what the Yoda of tennis had to say:

When you have a great second serve, you don't allow your opponent to take advantage of your missed first serve. If the second serve is weak, the opponent can step into it and punish you on the return. That's why people like Pete Sampras hit what seemed like two first serves. There wasn't really much of a distinction between his first and second serve, unlike in casual tennis.

There are basically two different types of second serves: the kick serve and the slice serve. It takes a little more effort to use a kick, or topspin, second serve because it requires a grip change. You have to toss the ball a little bit over the head and actually brush up and over the ball to get the ball to bounce up. If it's not a big enough topspin second serve, the ball sits up, and the opponent can take advantage of it.

The slice serve is effective because the ball stays low, thus forcing the returner to hit the ball up. It's often hit in the deuce court. The kick serve bounces up, into the body, making it difficult to return. Even though it's harder to master, young players should learn the kick serve. As they get older, they'll be able to hit it harder, which will be important as they move up the competitive ladder.

1. **The grip.** Hold the racket with the Continental grip. The player grips the handle as if grasping a hammer to hit a nail. The V formed by the thumb and index finger points to the first right-of-center ridge on the handle.

2. **The toss.** Your feet should be a foot or a foot and a half apart. Bring the arms up together. Some people, like Sampras, brought the tossing arm up, and then the racket arm sort of dragged behind. As a whole, it's easier to swing both arms together, for timing. If you're right-handed, bring the right elbow up high. It should be as high as the height of your shoulder. Your right elbow should be slightly bent, and then your racket drops behind your upper back. The left arm should extend as high as it can on the toss. Every great server always has that arm extended. For the second serve, the placement of the toss is a little bit more above your head. That way you can apply topspin by brushing up behind the ball.

3. **The coil.** Then you bend your knees. You rotate the hip slightly to your right while your knees push towards the right net post. You don't bend straight down, but you twist slightly towards the court. Your knees will be slightly more forward than your hips are. When you push your knees forward that way, your upper torso actually leans back a little bit. You end up in a position I always call the trophy position because most trophies given out to young players have a person just about to serve on the top. The racket then goes up behind your back with the racket face closed—that means the racket face is almost flat against your back.

4. **The launch.** Push up at the legs from the bent position and jump up and into the court with your left foot. Try to jump into the court about 12 inches. You could tell with both Sharapova and Pete Sampras how good their serve would be by how well they jumped up and into the court. If it was only a couple of inches, the serve was never good. So it's an important part of the serve to generate more power by jumping up and into the court. While you're pushing your legs up, you want to make contact with the ball on your way up—it adds to the power.

5. **The finish.** When you're about to land with your left foot into the court, you should kick your right leg up and back a little bit. Maria does it to an extreme—it's almost ridiculous to the extreme she does this—as does Marat Safin. It helps with the power if you time it right. Also, you stay in better balance.

One more thing:

You should also try to find a little bit of a ritual, like bounce the ball a certain number of times and adjust your hair. Something you do the same every time you serve. It relaxes you.

> **"It's one-on-one out there, man. There ain't no hiding. I can't pass the ball."**
> —Pete Sampras

MEASURE FOR MEASURE

WHAT THE QUARTERBACK RATING REALLY MEANS

The NFL's passer rating is an easy target for commentators and fans who are scared away by a system so intricate that the number for perfection is 158.3. But it's a useful measure of a quarterback's worth, so we're here to help you understand it. The calculation, devised by Don Smith of the Pro Football Hall of Fame in 1973, is based on four factors: percentage of completions per attempts, average yards gained per attempt, percentage of touchdown passes per attempt, and percentage of interceptions per attempt. Here's how to arrive at the number:

1. Take the passer's completion percentage, subtract 30, and multiply by .05. If the number falls between 0 and 2.375, the player gets that number. Numbers less than 0 get 0, and numbers greater than 2.375 get 2.375.

2. Take total yards passing, divide by attempts, subtract 3 from that number, and multiply the result by .25. Again, the minimum number you can get is 0, and the maximum is 2.375.

3. Take the number of TD passes, divide by attempts, and multiply by .20. The max is 2.375.

4. Divide the number of interceptions by passing attempts, and multiply that number by .25; then subtract the result from 2.375.

5. The four numbers are added, divided by 6, then multiplied by 100.

Got that? Don't worry if you're not following. As Steve Hirdt, executive vice president of the Elias Sports Bureau (the NFL's official statisticians), points out, "You may not know how outside air temperature is calculated, but you do know that when it's 10 degrees, you should

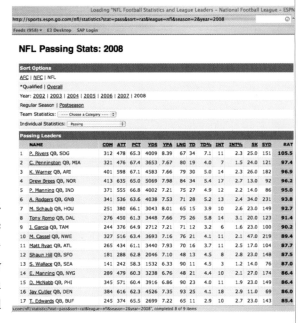

Loading "NFL Football Statistics and League Leaders - National Football League - ESPN

http://sports.espn.go.com/nfl/statistics?stat=pass&sort=rat&league=nfl&season=2&year=2008

Feeds (958) ▾ E3 Desktop SAP Login

NFL Passing Stats: 2008

Sort Options

AFC | NFC | NFL

*Qualified | Overall

Year: 2002 | 2003 | 2004 | 2005 | 2006 | 2007 | 2008

Regular Season | Postseason

Team Statistics: ---- Choose a Category ---- ◊

Individual Statistics: Passing ◊

Passing Leaders

	NAME	COM	ATT	PCT	YDS	YPA	LNG	TD	TD%	INT	INT%	SK	SYD	RAT
1	P. Rivers QB, SDG	312	478	65.3	4009	8.39	67	34	7.1	11	2.3	25.0	151	105.5
2	C. Pennington QB, MIA	321	476	67.4	3653	7.67	80	19	4.0	7	1.5	24.0	121	97.4
3	K. Warner QB, ARI	401	598	67.1	4583	7.66	79	30	5.0	14	2.3	26.0	182	96.9
4	Drew Brees QB, NOR	413	635	65.0	5069	7.98	84	34	5.4	17	2.7	13.0	92	96.2
5	P. Manning QB, IND	371	555	66.8	4002	7.21	75	27	4.9	12	2.2	14.0	86	95.0
6	A. Rodgers QB, GNB	341	536	63.6	4038	7.53	71	28	5.2	13	2.4	34.0	231	93.8
7	M. Schaub QB, HOU	251	380	66.1	3043	8.01	65	15	3.9	10	2.6	23.0	149	92.7
8	Tony Romo QB, DAL	276	450	61.3	3448	7.66	75	26	5.8	14	3.1	20.0	123	91.4
9	J. Garcia QB, TAM	244	376	64.9	2712	7.21	71	12	3.2	6	1.6	23.0	100	90.2
10	M. Cassel QB, NWE	327	516	63.4	3693	7.16	76	21	4.1	11	2.1	47.0	219	89.4
11	Matt Ryan QB, ATL	265	434	61.1	3440	7.93	70	16	3.7	11	2.5	17.0	104	87.7
12	Shaun Hill QB, SFO	181	288	62.8	2046	7.10	48	13	4.5	8	2.8	23.0	148	87.5
13	S. Wallace QB, SEA	141	242	58.3	1532	6.33	90	11	4.5	3	1.2	14.0	76	87.0
14	E. Manning QB, NYG	289	479	60.3	3238	6.76	48	21	4.4	10	2.1	27.0	174	86.4
15	D. McNabb QB, PHI	345	571	60.4	3916	6.86	90	23	4.0	11	1.9	23.0	149	86.4
16	Jay Cutler QB, DEN	384	616	62.3	4526	7.35	93	25	4.1	18	2.9	11.0	69	86.0
17	T. Edwards QB, BUF	245	374	65.5	2699	7.22	65	11	2.9	10	2.7	23.0	143	85.4

.com/nfl/statistics?stat=pass&sort=rat&league=nfl&season=2&year=2008", completed 8 of 9 items

> **"My only feeling about superstition is that it's unlucky to be behind at the end of a game."**
> —former Michigan State football coach Duffy Daugherty

wear a coat. TV executives may not know how the Nielsen ratings are computed, but they do know that *Desperate Housewives* is a winner."

But even Hirdt acknowledges that while the passer rating is an effective tool for measuring quarterbacks of the same era, it's unfair to use it to compare, say, Tom Brady with Johnny Unitas. Explains Hirdt, "There were many more deep passes in Unitas's time than there are today, so they had lower completion and higher interception rates. Consequently, most of the highest ratings belong to contemporary players."

That said, here are the best passers of all time, by season and career:

By Season		
Peyton Manning	121.1	2004
Tom Brady	117.2	2007
Steve Young	112.8	1994
Joe Montana	112.4	1989
Daunte Culpepper	110.9	2004

By Career		
Steve Young	96.8	1985–1999
Peyton Manning	94.7	1998–2008
Kurt Warner	93.8	1998–2008
Tom Brady	92.9	2000–2008
Joe Montana	92.3	1979–1994

PASS KEY
AN NFL QB GURU ON HOW TO THROW A SPIRAL

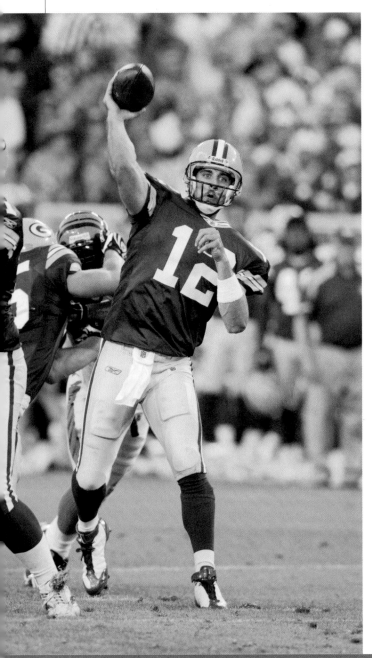

What **do** Aaron Rodgers, Kyle Boller, David Carr, Trent Dilfer, A. J. Feeley, Joey Harrington, Akili Smith, and Billy Volek have in common? Well, they've all been NFL quarterbacks. And they were all coached by Jeff Tedford.

Tedford, now the head coach at the University of California, is what you might call a quarterback guru. A former QB himself, Tedford set several career passing marks at Fresno State University and was named an honorable-mention All-America in 1982 when he threw for a school-record 2,993 yards and 24 touchdown passes.

After his playing career was over, Tedford coached QBs and became the offensive coordinator at his alma mater, then moved to the University of Oregon before he got the head job at Cal in 2002. He has been instrumental in developing six quarterbacks taken in the first round of the NFL draft, as well as two other NFL signal-callers. If anyone knows how to teach the mechanics of throwing a perfect spiral, it's Coach Tedford.

Packers quarterback Aaron Rodgers throws a pass against the Cincinnati Bengals at Lambeau Field.

"It all starts with the grip," says Tedford. "It has to feel comfortable."

Typically, the middle and ring fingers should be on the laces, he says, and then the placement of the index finger can vary. As for the thumb on the bottom of the ball, you have to make sure you're not palming the ball.

"If you hold the ball straight up and look between your thumb and your index finger, there should be some space, some daylight."

As far as throwing the ball goes, you don't want to grip it too tightly. There needs to be a pronation, or rotation, of the hand through the throwing process. The ball should come off the hand sequentially, with the pinky being the last finger to release.

Those are general tips for throwing a simple spiral. But becoming a truly consistent and efficient QB takes much more attention to detail. First comes ball placement.

"You should have two hands on the football," Tedford says, "held as if there was a shelf coming off of the top of the numbers on the jersey, with the ball pointed slightly outward.

"As you separate the ball, you want the elbow to be at least shoulder height. Then, as you release the ball coming through, you want the elbow to be eye level."

As for the follow-through, you want the throwing hand to end up in the opposite pocket. Tedford says it's important for the head to stay still, and you want to end with the shoulder underneath the chin.

Unless you work on the mechanics, the motion won't feel natural. One drill Coach Tedford recommends for younger players is to practice throwing the ball sitting only about eight to 10 yards apart with their legs spread. Then they should repeat the same drill on each knee, and then on both knees. This will simulate all the types of throws a QB makes.

When asked which member of his quarterback stable has the best mechanics, Tedford doesn't hesitate in picking out Rodgers.

"I think he's got a great career ahead of him," Tedford says.

In other words, he thinks he can throw long.

VINE YARD
THE STORY BEHIND THE IVY
AT WRIGLEY FIELD

It's called *Parthenocissus tricuspidata,* and Wrigley Field would not be Wrigley Field without it. Better known as Boston ivy, it was first planted at the base of the red brick wall for the new bleachers in 1937 at the behest of Bill Veeck, whose father was the Cubs' president. (Veeck also had fast-growing bittersweet strung from the top.) The effect of the East Asian vines was both ever changing—it's green in the summer and red-orange in the fall—and eternal. The ivy has become so synonymous with the Cubbies that the team's fan magazine is titled *Vine Line.*

Outfielders, however, don't have quite the same appreciation for the botanical wonder. For one thing, it does nothing to cushion the blow of the bricks hidden underneath. For another, it makes caroms unpredictable. But no outfielder hated the ivy as much as Lou Novikoff, who patrolled Wrigley in the 1940s. The Mad Russian actually thought it was poison ivy and would veer off on deep fly balls, thus infuriating his manager, Charlie Grimm. But then Novikoff was such a bad outfielder that even his wife, Esther, booed him. After he washed out of the majors, Novikoff became a star in fast-pitch softball, eventually making the

Groundskeepers plant the ivy at Wrigley Field, 1937.

Cubs left fielder Moises Alou leaps into the Wrigley Field ivy to make a catch against the White Sox, 2002.

International Softball Congress Hall of Fame. He died in 1970 and is buried in a leafy Los Angeles cemetery.

The ivy often snags baseballs and refuses to let them go—in which case, a ground-rule double is awarded. José Cardenal, an outfielder for the Cubs in the 1970s, tried to use that peculiarity to his advantage: He would hide baseballs in the vines so that he might quickly retrieve one and catch a runner unawares. Sounds crazy, but he did have 15 outfield assists in 1974.

In 2002, during a White Sox–Cubs series at Wrigley, a bleacher fan—no doubt from the South Side—poured acid on the vines in right center field, killing a section of ivy. But the grounds crew nursed the vines back to life, and now they are as robust as they've ever been. Bill Veeck would be proud. Lou Novikoff would be scared.

BAND LEADERS

THE FIVE GREATEST COLLEGE FIGHT SONGS

Collegefootball would not be as captivating as it is without the **marching band,** and the marching band would not be as stirring as it is without a signature song. So we asked David McKee, the longtime director of the Marching Virginians of Virginia Tech to name his five favorite fight songs. They are:

"The Victors" (University of Michigan). Written in 1898 by Louis Elbel, a Michigan student, and often known as "Hail to the Victors." John Philip Sousa himself called it "the greatest college fight song ever written."

"Notre Dame Victory March" (University of Notre Dame). Written in 1908 by Father Michael Shea and his brother, John, both Notre Dame grads, and first performed in their hometown of Holyoke, Massachusetts. The song has some great lines, including "Wake up the echoes cheering her name" and "Shake down the thunder from the sky." Even if you don't like the Fighting Irish, you can't help but "cheer, cheer for old Notre Dame."

"Fight On!" (University of Southern California). Composed by a dental student named Milo Sweet in 1922 for a spirit competition. The song was used to inspire troops in the Aleutian campaign in World War II.

The Michigan Marching Band performs for the home crowd at Michigan Stadium in Ann Arbor, 2006.

"Across the Field" (Ohio State University). Band members indeed "set the Earth reverberating" with this song, and the players sing it after every game. It dates back to 1915, and on the band's website you can hear the composer, William Dougherty Jr. play it himself.

"Washington and Lee Swing" (Washington and Lee University). What's a small-school song doing in a big-school list? Well, written in 1910 by three alumni, not only was it copied by many schools, but it also became a standard for such musicians as Pete Fountain, Red Nichols, Glenn Miller, and Louis Armstrong.

By the way, you haven't lived until you've seen the tuba section of the Marching Virginians perform the Hokie Pokey.

Good choices: In the 1965 NFL draft, the Chicago Bears selected both Gale Sayers and Dick Butkus in the first round.

UNDERHANDED WAYS

If you've ever played competitive fast-pitch softball, you know that hitting a softball 12 inches in circumference thrown from 40 feet away is just as difficult as hitting a hardball 9 inches in circumference thrown from 60 feet, 6 inches away. And one of the people who has made softball especially hard is pitcher Michele Smith, who has twice won Olympic gold medals for the United States and now plays professionally in Japan.

In her own words, here's a look inside Smith's ball bag of tricks:

Rise Ball

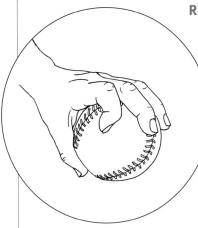

Spin. The ball should spin backward and rise up through the strike zone. I cock my wrist backward and underneath the ball. My pinky finger is the closest finger toward the batter when I spin the ball backward as I release it. The spin has the same effect as an airplane: It will cause a decrease in pressure underneath the seams, which will cause the pitch to rise.

Speed. I throw this pitch fast. As the velocity increases, so does the ball movement.

Grip. There are a few different ways to grip the ball, but I place my middle finger on the top seam, my ring finger on the bottom seam, and tuck in my index and pinky fingers. My thumb is opposite my middle finger.

> **Bobby Richardson is the only second baseman and the only player from the losing team to win the World Series MVP (1960).**

Curveball

Spin. The ball should spin like a top in a circular rotation and move from side to side. For a right-handed pitcher, the ball will move away from a right-handed batter. For a left-handed pitcher, like me, the ball will move in to a right-handed hitter. I snap my wrist around the ball as I release it, rotate my hand sideways, and pull the ball across my body in one swift motion.

Speed. The velocity should be a bit slower than that of a fastball, to give it time to curve.

Grip. I grip the curve exactly like the rise ball but rotate the ball just a little bit so that I am sliding my middle finger up on the smile formed by the top of the seams. Again, my ring finger is on the bottom.

> **Dutch Levsen pitched complete-game victories (6–1, 5–1) in both ends of a 1926 doubleheader between his Cleveland Indians and the Boston Red Sox.**

Drop Ball

Spin. The ball should spin over the top, or spin forward with a downward rotation, and move from high to low. It's almost like an overhand curve in baseball. I snap downward as I release the ball and rotate my hand over the ball with my thumb leading the ball initially but ending up on the bottom once I have finished my rotation.

Speed. The velocity should be a bit slower than that of a fastball—it needs time to drop.

Grip. I place all three fingers over the top seams, thumb opposite the middle finger, and tuck in my pinky.

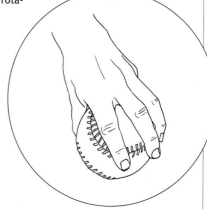

Changeup

Spin. The best changeups have a tight spin either like a curve or backward for a flip changeup. The faster the ball spins, the harder it is for the batter to read that the pitch is actually slower than a fastball.

Speed. At least 25 percent slower than a fastball. But because the object is to fool the batter, look as explosive off the mound as you would with a fastball.

Grip. There are a lot of different grips. I like to start out with my rise-ball grip. But I hold the ball deeper in the palm of my hand, tuck in a finger so it looks like a regular rise ball, then put all my fingers on the ball.

Knuckleball

Spin. Not many pitchers throw the knuckler. It is difficult to master and control and tough for a catcher to handle. The trick is to throw it with *no* spin: The ball floats and moves in random, unpredictable directions.

Speed. At least 25 percent slower than a fastball—the slower, the better. But just like the changeup, you want the batter to think you're throwing a fastball.

Grip. My fingers are bent against the ball so the knuckles of my fingers are against the ball. The ball is deep in the palm of my hand—that helps me lock my wrist so there is no wrist snap and consequently no spin. As I release the ball, I take my thumb off and let the ball float out of my hand.

Calvin Coolidge is the only president to attend more than one game in a single World Series: He went to games 1, 6, and 7 in Washington in 1924.

MIGHTIEST GAME (HOCKEY)

WHY THE MIRACLE ON ICE WASN'T REALLY

Eleven seconds, you're got 10 seconds, the countdown is going on right now! Morrow, up to Silk . . . five seconds left in the game. Do you believe in miracles? Yes!"

Even if you weren't around to hear Al Michaels's call, you probably know that was his description of the waning moments of the United States Olympic hockey team's 4–3 victory over the Soviet Union on February 22, 1980. The so-called Miracle on Ice is unquestionably the most famous hockey game ever played, but to call it a "miracle" does a disservice to the 20 American collegians who poured seven months of their lives into those Oympics and to the man who forged their gold medal.

Heck, the real miracle was that Herb Brooks wasn't replaced as the coach before Lake Placid. He regularly defied his bosses at USA Hockey, he tormented his players to the edge of revolt, and when the U.S. lost

> In *Miracle,* **the 2004 movie about the Miracle on Ice, Buzz Schneider is played by his son, Billy.**

10–3 to the U.S.S.R. in a February 9 exhibition, he came under attack from the media.

But right from the beginning, Brooks had a plan. A successful coach at the University of Minnesota, he picked players for their intelligence and their willingness to challenge assumptions because he was going to teach them a new style of play. He talked to track and swimming coaches before designing a rigorous conditioning program that made the Americans the best-conditioned athletes on the ice—they outscored their Olympic opponents 16–3 in the third period. And, somewhat against his nature, he made himself the bad guy, preferring to unite his players in fear of him rather than in fear of the Russians.

When not subjecting his players to "Herbies"—those all-out sprints at the end of each practice—he hit them with such Brooks-isms as "You're playing worse every day, and right now you're playing like the middle of next month," and "Gentlemen, you don't have enough talent to win on talent alone." Brooks died in 2003, but if you've seen Kurt Russell play him in the 2004 movie *Miracle,* you have a pretty good idea of what he was like: E. M. Swift of *Sports Illustrated,* who knew Brooks well and chronicled the team so beautifully back in 1980, called the performance "hauntingly true-to-life."

The defining goal of the Olympics was actually the goal that tied the Russians 2–2 in the first period. With only seconds left in the period, defenseman Dave Christian took a 100-foot slap shot that goaltender Vladislav Tretiak let rebound off his pads. He and his teammates thought the period was over, but center Mark Johnson (who had been battling with Brooks) flew to the net, weaving through two Soviet defenders. He feinted a shot, pulling Tretiak to his knees, then veered left and slid the puck behind Tretiak. It was a combination of Soviet overconfidence and American hustle, and it resulted in the U.S.S.R. coach replacing Tretiak, the best goalie in the world, with his backup, Vladimir Myshkin.

Suddenly the Russians looked mortal, and even though the U.S. fell behind 3–2 in the second period, Jim Craig made save after save until Johnson tied it up in the third period. Then, with 10 minutes left in the game, captain and left wing Mike Eruzione happened upon a loose puck and fired it through a screen past Myshkin for a 4-3 lead. Disoriented, the Russians started playing like the teams who usually panicked against them.

Still, the Americans needed to beat Finland two days later to claim the gold, which they did, 4–2, for their first Olympic gold since Squaw Valley in 1960. Herb Brooks was the last forward cut from that team, which made his victory in Lake Placid that much sweeter.

Knowing what that last cut felt like made it especially hard for Brooks to give the news to the last forward he cut, Ralph Cox, a few days before the Olympics. As Brooks told Swift later that year, "He was such a gentleman that I cried on it. I had a little flashback of myself at the time. And you know what he told me? True story. He said, 'That's all right, coach, I understand. You guys are going to win the gold medal.' *Ralph Cox* said that. And when we won it, that's who I thought of. Ralph Cox."

OPPOSITE PAGE:

Miracle on Ice: Team USA celebrates after defeating the USSR 4–3 in the Olympic semifinal on February 22, 1980.

REAL SORRY MISSING THE TRIPLE CROWN BY A NOSE

I n the chart below, you will see the 11 horses that came this close to winning thoroughbred racing's Triple Crown since Affirmed won the last one, in 1978: They took the Kentucky Derby and the Preakness but failed in the Belmont. And one of them, Real Quiet, lost the Belmont by a nose.

Horse	Year	Belmont Result
Spectacular Bid	1979	3rd
Pleasant Colony	1981	3rd
Alysheba	1987	4th
Sunday Silence	1989	2nd (8 lengths)
Silver Charm	1997	2nd (¾ length)
Real Quiet	1998	2nd (nose)
Charismatic	1999	3rd
War Emblem	2002	8th
Funny Cide	2003	3rd
Smarty Jones	2004	2nd
Big Brown	2008	9th

Too bad about Real Quiet because he was a movie in the making. A Colombian horseman, Eduardo Gaviria, had carefully bred his stallion, Really Blue, to the mare Quiet American, but the colt's knees were so crooked that Gaviria sold Real Quiet at a yearling auction to Michael Pegram for a mere $17,000. Trained by Bob Baffert, Real Quiet didn't get his first win until his seventh race as a two-year-old. Even though he won the Hollywood Futurity, Real Quiet wasn't given much of a chance to win the Derby and was in fact considered second fiddle to Baffert's other entry, Indian Charlie. For edging out Victory Gallop by a half-length in the Derby, Real Quiet paid a rather loud $18.80.

Real Quiet again defeated Victory Gallop in the Preakness, by a more comfortable two and a half lengths. According to a pre-Belmont story in *The New York*

Times, "When his cargo plane landed at Kennedy Airport . . . , the wing door swung open and the chief members of the cast—the owner, Mike Pegram; the trainer, Bob Baffert, and the jockey, Kent Desormeaux—stood there with index fingers over their mouths, signifying 'real quiet.'" Desormeaux said he was "98 percent sure of winning."

With two furlongs to go in the 1½-mile Belmont, Real Quiet opened up a four-length lead. But Victory Gallop closed fast on the outside, and though Desormeaux angled his horse out, the two horses arrived at the wire at the same moment. After five minutes, the results were announced: Victory Gallop by a nose. As it turned out, had Real Quiet crossed the wire first, he would not have won. Said Belmont steward John Joyce, "There was some significant lugging out there. We probably would have D.Q.'d [disqualified] Real Quiet if he had won."

Victory Gallop edges out favorite Real Quiet in a photo finish at the Belmont Stakes on June 6, 1998, denying Real Quiet the Triple Crown by the narrowest of margins.

ACE OF CLUBS THE MASTER OF THE HOLE IN ONE

It's a once-in-a-lifetime thrill that Norman Manley has experienced 59 times. It's something Rhiannon Linacre did when she was 9 years, 75 days old and Elsie McLean did when she was 102. It's the great equalizer, a shot that links hackers to the greats of the game.

We're talking, of course, about the hole in one, and one person who can talk about it is West Texan Mancil Davis, the so-called King of Aces and the official PGA record holder, with 51 of them. Says Davis, "You'll never be as good as Tiger Woods, but anyone can hit a hole in one just like Tiger."

Davis says that his aces have come in all forms: "the good, the bad, and the ugly." One of his favorites came when his ball hit a tree and a sprinkler head before finding its way into the cup. Another time, he was giving a couple a playing lesson when he demonstrated the ball right into the hole. Here are three tips from the King:

1. **Visualize the shot.** For years, I always said that I felt differently on a par 3. I'm a big believer in visualization. And a par 3 is just a visual hole.
2. **Aim at the hole.** I ask golfers what they are aiming for on a par 3, and very few of them say the hole. That will help you visualize the ball rolling into the hole.
3. **Use enough club.** It's typical for players to underclub, but that's because they don't know how long they hit their clubs. Most golfers aren't as strong as they are in their minds. So be honest with yourself.

In case you're wondering, Tiger has 19 holes in one, which gives him one more than Jack Nicklaus but 26 fewer than one-time PGA golfer Art Wall.

> Apollo 14 astronaut Alan Shepard is the only man to hit a golf ball on the moon. Because the suit was so bulky, he could use only one arm, and it took him three swings to connect solidly with his makeshift six-iron, but the ball went an estimated 240 yards.

"Let your attitude determine your golf game. Don't let your golf game determine your attitude."
—golfer Davis Love Jr.

OPPOSITE PAGE:

Tiger Woods celebrates his hole in one during the Par 3 Contest at Augusta National Golf Club in Augusta, Georgia, April 7, 2004.

MIGHTIEST GAME (BASKETBALL)
THE NIGHT WILT CHAMBERLAIN SCORED 100

In the early morning hours of March 2, 1962, Wilt Chamberlain closed up his nightclub in Harlem, Small's Paradise, and caught a train to Philadelphia, where he was to meet his Warrior teammates for a bus ride to Hershey, Pennsylvania, to play a game against the New York Knicks. Back in those days, the Warriors would occasionally play a game at the Hershey Arena, a two-hour ride from Philadelphia. "We arrived at the arena at 3:30," Wilt wrote in his book *A View from Above.* "I spent the rest of the time before the game shooting a rifle at a penny arcade. I completely destroyed all existing shooting records there—an omen of things to come."

He was hot, all right. Playing in front of just 4,124 fans, Wilt had 23 points in the first quarter, 18 in the second. Jim Heffernan, who covered the game for the Philadelphia *Bulletin,* recalled, "That was no big deal to us because he had 78 earlier in the season. What we did notice was that he was making his free throws." Chamberlain, a notoriously horrible foul shooter, had made 13 of 14 in the first half.

It wasn't like the Knicks were lying down for Chamberlain. The two teams actively disliked each other. But he scored another 28 points in the third quarter. To try to keep him in check, the Knicks started holding the ball, milking the 24 seconds they were allowed on each possession. The Warriors, for their part, kept feeding the ball to Wilt. Here's the call of Bill Campbell, the WCAU broadcaster:

He has 98 with 1:01 left, he can make it easily. . . . Rodgers in to Chamberlain, misses, Luckenbill rebound, back to Ruklick, in to Chamberlain . . . he made it! A dipper dunk! He made it! They've stopped the game. The fans are all over the floor. One hundred points for Wilt Chamberlain!

In the locker room afterward, Wilt was asked to pose holding a sheet of paper with *100* written on it. But that was the extent of the celebration. As teammate Al Attles remembered, "Sweat dripping off him, a glass of milk in one hand, . . . he's

> "They say that nobody is perfect. Then they tell you practice makes perfect. I wish they'd make up their minds."
>
> —Wilt Chamberlain

shaking his head. 'What's the matter, big fella?' I asked him. And he said, 'I never thought I'd take 63 shots.' To which I said, 'Yeah, but you made 36 of them!'"

After the game, Chamberlain hitched a ride back to New York with some of the Knicks. When they let him off, Wilt told them, "You guys are sure nice to this SOB. Letting me score a hundred points, then giving me a ride all the way back to my apartment."

AIR BALLS
THE FAMILY SECRETS OF THE WIFFLE BALL

Back in 1953, David J. Mullany's father had a problem. While throwing curveballs with a plastic golf ball in his Connecticut backyard, his arm had become sore. So *his* father, David N. Mullany, a failed auto-polish salesman, came to the rescue, inventing and then producing the light plastic orb now known as the Wiffle ball. Today, the sport it bred is played all over the map, across the demographic spectrum.

Now the president of Wiffle Ball, Inc., in Shelton, Connecticut, David J. Mullany says that there are infinite ways of throwing the ball, based on different arm angles and the direction in which the holes are facing on release. But Mullany offers up his three favorite pitches, based on experience:

1. **Curveball.** The right-handed Mullany prefers to hold the ball with the perforations facing left, throwing it either overhead or from a three-quarter release, with his arm at a 45-degree angle. That way, the ball curves away from a right-hander. If he wants the ball to curve in to the batter, he simply flips the ball so the holes face to the right.

2. **Riser.** Hold the ball so the indentations face the ground. Throw this pitch with your arm between three quarters and sidearm, and watch as the ball rises up toward the batter before the bottom drops out and the ball loses momentum.

3. **Knuckleball.** Just like Tim Wakefield's floater, this pitch ducks and dives, with varying results. The holes should face your palm, with your index, middle, and ring fingers just inside the perforations. Throw it straight overhand, and push outward with your fingers. If you release it correctly, the ball won't spin, and it'll bewilder the heck out of your opponent.

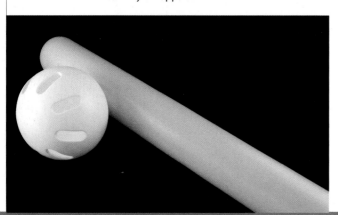

In other words, those are the pitches that will put the whiff in Wiffle ball.

COLOR FAST
WHY THE TOUR DE FRANCE LEADER WEARS YELLOW

The yellow jersey worn by the leader of the Tour de France is one of the most recognizable symbols in all of sports. But there is an ongoing debate about when *le maillot jaune* was first worn, and by whom.

The first Tour winners wore a green armband. Belgian rider Philippe Thys took credit for being the first to wear the yellow when he won the race in 1913, saying he wished to wear a bright color that both set him off from the crowd and served as an advertisement for his Peugeot racing team. All of which may be true, but there are no accounts or witnesses to corroborate the claim.

Lance Armstrong leads the pack during Stage 14 (Draguignan to Briançon) of the Tour de France, July 15, 2000.

The more widely accepted story credits Frenchman Eugène Christophe, who wore a yellow jersey during the Grenoble-to-Geneva stage to reflect the color of *L'Auto,* the newspaper that organized the event. At the time, tour organizer Henri Desgrange wrote: "This morning I gave the valiant Christophe a superb yellow jersey.... Our director decided that the man leading the race should wear a jersey in the colors of *L'Auto.* The battle to wear this jersey is going to be passionate."

While those words proved to be prophetic, Christophe came to hate the color. He complained that spectators and riders alike teased him and imitated canaries during the whole course: "Ah, the yellow jersey! Isn't he a beautiful canary?"

Funny, Lance Armstrong had no problem with it.

ALL THE RAGE
THE FIVE BEST (OR WORST) SPORTS TANTRUMS

Because pro sports are played at such a high level of intensity, players and coaches often let their emotions get the best of them. Whereas such eruptions may lead to fines and suspensions for those involved, they provide plenty of excitement and entertainment for the average sports fan. Here are five of the best (or worst?) on-field temper tantrums:

John McEnroe. The Godfather of Gripe may hold the record for the most blowups. His most memorable moment of rage still rings loudly in fans' ears. En route to his first-ever Wimbledon title in 1981, John McEnroe disagreed with the umpire's ruling during his first-round match with Tom Gullikson. Citing the chalk that supposedly "flew up" as the ball hit the line, he tore into the chair umpire, roaring the now famous words, *"You cannot be serious!"* McEnroe went on to argue, "Everyone knows it's in, in this whole stadium, and you call that out?" and concluded, "You guys are the absolute pits of the world."

Phillip Wellman. The manager of the Class AA Mississippi Braves made a name for himself and a video for the ages on June 1, 2007, in a game against the Chattanooga Lookouts. Phillip Wellman was not pleased with a particular call by the home plate umpire and was ejected while arguing from the dugout. He came charging onto the field, slamming his cap to the ground, and getting so close to the umpire's face that he could have kissed him. But Wellman clearly wasn't in an affectionate mood. His ensuing antics included covering home plate entirely with dirt (drawing the outline of a new, much bigger one to illustrate his point), chucking third base into center field, and imitating all of the umpires in a less than flattering manner. The most creative portion of Wellman's performance came when he dropped to the ground and crawled toward the pitcher's mound, finally grabbing the rosin bag and tossing it, grenade-style, at the home plate umpire's feet. After a few more sardonic gestures, Wellman made his way off the field (taking second and third base with him) and exited to a raucous ovation. And the Braves weren't even the home team.

Eric Cantona. Admittedly, angry outbursts don't always end well for the fans. During a 1995 regular-season match against Crystal Palace, Manchester United forward Eric Cantona was shown his fifth red card since joining the English powerhouse, and he was not happy about it. Rather than take his frustration out on the referee who sent him off, he chose to channel his rage in a different direction. As he was being escorted off the field, Cantona flew toward the stands, landing a kung-fu-style kick on the chest of a Palace supporter while throwing a few punches for good measure. Cantona's intentions were never determined. When asked about the incident, he was cryptic at best, offering, "When the seagulls follow the trawler, it's because they think sardines will be thrown into the sea."

Bob Knight. An entire list could be devoted to Bobby Knight tantrums. One, however, will forever live on in sports infamy. During a 1985 game against Purdue, Knight received a technical foul for protesting a call. As Purdue guard Steve Reed was setting up for the free throw, Knight staged another protest, this time launching his chair across the court, nearly hitting Reed. Knight was given a one-game suspension and two years' probation. Bobby seemed to have something against people named Reed: He once choked Neil Reed, one of his own Indiana players.

Indiana coach Bobby Knight winds up and throws a chair across the floor during Indiana's 72–63 loss to Purdue on February 23, 1985.

Jim Schoenfeld. After his Devils lost to the Bruins, 6–1, in game 3 of the 1988 Stanley Cup semifinals, coach Jim Schoenfeld took out his frustration on referee Don Koharski. The coach followed Koharski toward the officials' dressing rooms, ripping him and the rest of his crew. During the fracas, Koharski fell down, blaming Schoenfeld (who had to be restrained) and yelling that Schoenfeld would never coach again, to which the coach eloquently replied, "That's 'cause you fell, you fat pig! Have another doughnut! Have another doughnut!" Schoenfeld was suspended for the next game but got a court order overturning the suspension, a move that instigated a boycott by the game 4 referees, who refused to officiate with Schoenfeld on the bench. The league was forced to use local refs for the game. Schoenfeld would later be suspended for the incident—with no court order to protect him.

MAKING WAVES

American Olympic gold medalist Gertrude Ederle enters the water for her cross-Channel swim on August 7, 1926.

The ticker tape parade for her drew 2 million spectators. They wrote songs about her, invited her to the White House, and put her in a short movie about herself. Heywood Broun wrote of her, "It may be that she will turn out to be an even greater discoverer than Columbus—it was only a continent which he found."

She was Gertrude Ederle, and on August 6, 1926, the 19-year-old became the first woman to swim across the English Channel, entering the water at Cap Gris-Nez, Pas-de-Calais, France, at 7:05 A.M. and coming ashore at Kingsdown, Kent, England, at 9:35 P.M. Her time of 14:31 was 2 hours better than the previous best.

The daughter of a Manhattan butcher, she had thrown herself into swimming after a near drowning in her youth. A product of the Women's Swimming Association, the club that also produced Eleanor Holm and Esther Williams, Ederle won three medals in the 1924 Paris Olympics, including a gold in the 400-meter freestyle relay. She had made an attempt at swimming the Channel in August of 1925, but her trainer pulled her out of the water against her will.

While other women were planning and training for their own attempts, Ederle found a new trainer, Thomas Burgess, for her second try. She also donned a revolutionary two-piece bathing suit, designed by her older sister, Margaret; slathered herself in sheep grease; and wore goggles kept tight to her face with candle wax. Braving the choppy seas, she would occasionally sing "Let Me Call You Sweetheart" to the rhythm of her crawl stroke. Crew members on the accompanying boat would urge her along by holding up signs saying "One Wheel" and "Two Wheels," to remind her of the new roadster she had been promised. During her 12th hour at sea, Burgess was so worried about the unfavorable winds that he shouted, "Gertie, you must come out!" Ederle raised her head from the water and replied, "What for?"

By one reckoning, Ederle ended up swimming 35 miles to make the 21-mile crossing. Waiting on the other side were hundreds of people, some with flares. Years later she would recall, "When I walked out of the water, I began thinking, 'Oh my God, have I really done it?' When my feet hit the sand, oh, that was a wonderful moment." A British passport official approached and jokingly asked for her papers.

A week later, Ederle returned home on the steamship *Berengaria,* and as the ship entered New York Harbor, she was asked to go to the top deck. She recalled, "I went up there. The planes circled around and swooped down and dropped those bouquets. They were just gorgeous."

After the parade, the visit with President Coolidge, the obligatory vaudeville tour, the song ("Tell Me Trudy, Who Is Going to Be the Lucky One?"), the movie (*Swim Girl, Swim*), . . . came—well—if not tragedy, then obscurity. Her manager frittered away her money. Her fiancé ditched her when he discovered that her hearing, weakened by a childhood bout of measles, had gotten worse from all that swimming. She suffered a nervous breakdown. She slipped on some tiles in a stairwell in 1933, injuring her spine and bringing on constant pain.

But she simply went on with her life, living in Queens, New York, working at La Guardia Airport, teaching deaf children to swim. "Since I can't hear, either," she said, "they feel I'm one of them."

She died in a New Jersey nursing home at the age of 98. Before she went, she said, "I am not a person who reaches for the moon as long as I have the stars. God has been good to me."

It's time for another movie about Gertrude Ederle.

TAKE A HIKE
A LONG SNAPPER ON WHY IT'S NOT A SNAP

Combine the loneliness of the long-distance runner with the arcane routines of the knuckleball pitcher and the masochism of the sparring partner, and you have . . . the long snapper. Taken for granted until he screws up, the long snapper—the man responsible for hiking the ball to the punter or the holder in football—is a special breed. Rob Davis is one.

Back when he was a 17-year-old defensive lineman at Eleanor Roosevelt High School in Greenbelt, Maryland, Davis practiced long snapping with an almost farcical devotion. He did the same at Pennsylvania's Shippensburg University and used the skill to become the first Shippensburg player to make the NFL. After failed attempts to land a job with the New York Jets, Kansas City Chiefs, Pittsburgh Steelers, and Chicago Bears, Davis caught a lucky break in 1997 when Green Bay's starting long snapper, Paul Frase, injured his back.

At the time of his retirement, 10 years later, Davis had played in 167 straight games, placing him third all-time on the Packers' list of players in consecutive games, behind Forrest Gregg and Brett Favre. Now the director of player development for the Pack, Davis admits to just three bad snaps. He says, "Long snapping is the job everybody thinks they can do—except on Sundays. As a defensive lineman, you can miss a tackle and get another set of downs. This margin of error does not exist for our kind."

As the long snapper first lines up, his quadriceps, triceps, and back start to tense, coiling the necessary springs to snap the ball to the holder or the punter. Gripping the ball with both hands, he lets fly a picture-perfect spiral—upside down! In regard to hand position, Davis says it varies from center to center: "Guys hold the ball differently, just like throwing a football. As for myself, I never had my hand on the laces because I felt more comfortable and better able to control the rise of the football."

When the holder or the punter calls for the football, the snap hand (the hand used to throw the football) and the guide hand break simultaneously in a whiplike motion. The level of the guide

> On September 21, 1969, Jets rookie punter Steve O'Neal got off the longest punt in NFL history, 98 yards, from the Jets' one-yard line to the Denver Broncos' one-yard line.

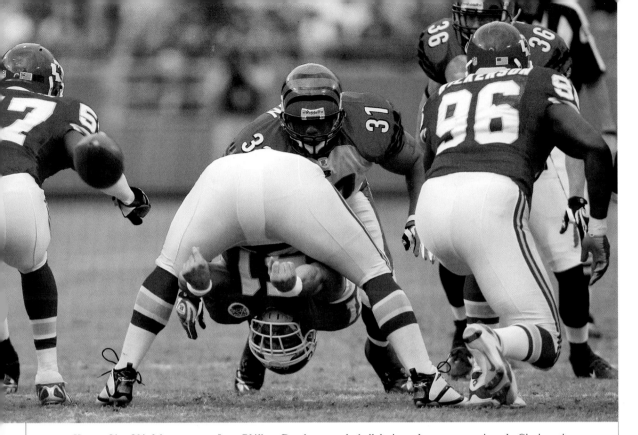

Kansas City Chiefs long snapper Jean-Philippe Darche snaps the ball during a home game against the Cincinnati Bengals at Arrowhead Stadium on October 14, 2007.

hand is key, since this hand directs the ball's path. With a 10-yard punt snap, the guide hand should be level with the punter's crotch, but for a 6-yard field goal attempt the guide hand should be level with the holder's biceps. It is essential that long snappers practice from different angles and parts of the field to better control accuracy. Says Davis, "On Sundays, I would go out with either the punter or the kicker and his holder and practice about 12 punts and 20 to 30 field goals from different spots."

That's actually the easy part. Once the ball is released, "guys are immediately on you," says Davis. "Teams rush fairly quickly, with linebackers ready to block the ball." Thus, the hardest job of a long snapper is to quickly ready his hands, previously between his legs, to block 300-plus pounds of force. "You have to keep guys from traveling 10 yards for a two count until the ball is in the air."

And if you don't? Well, that's when a long snapper will find himself with his tail between his legs.

ROLL THE DICE
STRAT-O-MATIC'S ALL-TIME BASEBALL TEAM

There are gods who walk among us. **Mariano Rivera.** LeBron James. Tom Brady. Harold Richman.

If you're unfamiliar with Mr. Richman, he is the inventor of Strat-O-Matic Baseball. If you do know who he is, then you also know that he has given pleasure to millions while taking countless man-hours from schools, workplaces, and families. He came up with his dice simulation of baseball when he was 11 years old, in 1952, and began selling it out of his parents' basement 10 years later.

Now there are Strat-O-Matic versions for the NFL, the NBA, and the NHL, as well as cards covering most of baseball history. Among the game's devotees are Spike Lee, George W. Bush, Tim Robbins, Drew Carey, a host of sportscasters and sportswriters, and a fair number of people who actually have cards of their own, like Cal Ripken Jr., Dale Murphy, and Keith Hernandez.

The baseball game and Richman are still going strong. We asked him for his all-time Strat-O-Matic team, his go-to guys for the times when he goes to play his own game. Here they are, with fielding and speed ratings for the position players:

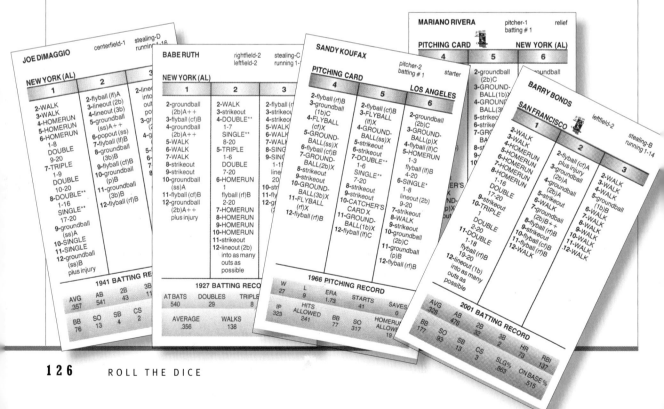

Position, Player, Team	Stat Highlights	Fielding	Speed
C Yogi Berra, 1950 Yankees	.322, 124 RBIs	2	D 1-13
C Johnny Bench, 1972 Reds	40 HRs, 125 RBIs	1	D 1-12
1B Lou Gehrig, 1927 Yankees	.373, 47 HRs, 175 RBIs	2	C 1-13
1B Mark McGwire,* 1998 Cards	70 HRs, 147 RBIs	3	E 1-8
2B Rogers Hornsby, 1924 Cards	.424, 25 HRs	2	D 1-15
2B Charlie Gehringer, 1934 Tigers	.356, 127 RBIs	1	B 1-15
SS Ernie Banks, 1957 Cubs	43 HRs, 34 doubles	2	C 1-15
SS Cal Ripken Jr., 1991 Orioles	.323, 34 HRs, 46 doubles	1	D 1-13
3B Mike Schmidt, 1980 Phillies	48 HRs, 121 RBIs	1	A 1-14
3B Wade Boggs, 1987 Red Sox	.363, 24 HRs	2	E 1-12
LF Ted Williams, 1941 Red Sox	.406, 37 HRs, 120 RBIs	3	D 1-13
LF Barry Bonds,* 2001 Giants	73 HRs, .515 OBP	2	B 1-14
CF Willie Mays, 1954 Giants	.345, 41 HRs, 13 triples	1	C 1-17
CF Ty Cobb, 1911 Tigers	.420, 24 triples, 83 SBs	1	AA 1-17
RF Babe Ruth, 1927 Yankees	.356, 60 HRs, 164 RBIs	2	C 1-14
RF Hank Aaron, 1957 Braves	.322, 44 HRs, 132 RBIs	1	D 1-14
DH Joe DiMaggio, 1941 Yankees	.357, 43 doubles, 13 Ks	CF-1	D 1-16
DH Stan Musial, 1948 Cardinals	.376, 39 HRs, 46 doubles	LF-2, 1B-2	C 1-14
RHP Bob Gibson, 1968 Cardinals	22-9, 1.12 ERA, 13 ShOs		
RHP Pedro Martinez, 1999 Red Sox	23-4, 2.07 ERA, 313 Ks		
LHP Sandy Koufax, 1966 Dodgers	27-9, 1.73 ERA, 317 Ks		
LHP Ron Guidry, 1978 Yankees	25-3, 1.74 ERA, 248 Ks		
rel. Mariano Rivera, 2005 Yankees	43 saves, 1.38 ERA		
rel. Bruce Sutter, 1984 Cardinals	45 saves, 1.54 ERA		

If you're wondering why McGwire's and Bonds's names have asterisks—well, then you haven't been following along.

> After being asked by general manager Branch Rickey to keep the terms of his contract a secret, Dodgers pitcher Billy Loes replied, "Don't worry, I'm just as ashamed of the figures as you are."

YOGI BERRA catcher-2 steal...
NEW YORK YANKEES runni... 13

> "Man may penetrate the outer reaches of the universe, he may solve the very secret of eternity itself, but for me, the ultimate human experience is to witness the flawless execution of a hit-and-run."
> —Branch Rickey

BOOK MARKS

FIVE REASONS SPORTS LITERATURE ISN'T AN OXYMORON

Forests have been felled to feed the market for sports books, and there is no shortage of good ones out there. But to narrow the field, and to risk folly, we asked Daniel Okrent, the acclaimed author of *Nine Innings* and *Public Editor #1,* to name the five sports books he would take to a desert island. Here is his selection:

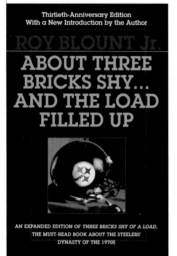

Thirtieth-Anniversary Edition
With a New Introduction by the Author

ROY BLOUNT Jr.
ABOUT THREE BRICKS SHY... AND THE LOAD FILLED UP

AN EXPANDED EDITION OF *THREE BRICKS SHY OF A LOAD,*
THE MUST-READ BOOK ABOUT THE STEELERS'
DYNASTY OF THE 1970S

About Three Bricks Shy of a Load by **Roy Blount Jr.** Blount spent a season with the 1973 Pittsburgh Steelers, on the verge of their dynasty. Here he is on training camp: " '*Yunh. Yunh,* nng*Oomph.*' It is strange and a little unnerving to hear this sort of thing for most of a morning or afternoon while watching people spit and lunge and blow their noses in their hands and heave against each other over and over again, doing the fundamental things repeatedly, not for the immediate purpose of advancing or stopping a drive, but for the sake of the fundamental things. It was something like watching a pornographic movie."

Ball Four by **Jim Bouton.** The journeyman pitcher wove anecdotes from his career into a diary of his 1969 season with the Seattle Pilots and Houston Astros and gave us this classic description of a meeting he had with manager Joe Schultz: "At the precise moment I started to explain why I thought I needed more work, Joe Schultz took a huge bite out of the liverwurst sandwich he was eating, got up off his stool, went to the Coke machine and mumbled something to me through his full mouth over his shoulder. I didn't pitch. That's how I know what he said."

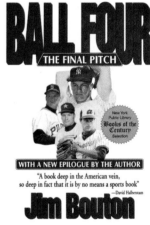

BALL FOUR
THE FINAL PITCH

New York
Public Library
Books of the
Century
Selection

WITH A NEW EPILOGUE BY THE AUTHOR
"A book deep in the American vein,
so deep in fact that it is by no means a sports book"
—David Halberstam
Jim Bouton

> Snuffy Stirnweiss, a Yankee outfielder who won the 1945 American League batting title, died at the age of 40 when his New Jersey commuter train plunged off a bridge after the motorman suffered a heart attack.

The Sweet Science by A. J. Liebling. This compilation of the great writer's boxing pieces transports you to a world that's brutal and noble and poetic. Talking about the practice of putting sparring partners on the undercard, Liebling wrote, "Sparring partners are endowed with habitual consideration and forbearance, and they find it hard to change character. A kind of guild fellowship holds them together, and they pepper each other's elbows with merry abandon, grunting with pleasure like hippopotamuses in a beer vat."

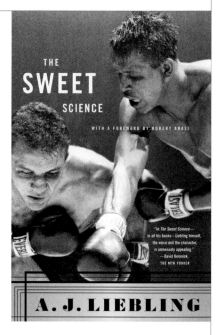

The Summer Game by Roger Angell. The first of Angell's collections covers the years 1962–72 and sets an impossibly high standard for any baseball writer other than Angell himself: "Since baseball time is measured only in outs, all you have to do is succeed utterly; keep hitting, keep the rally alive, and you have defeated time. You remain forever young."

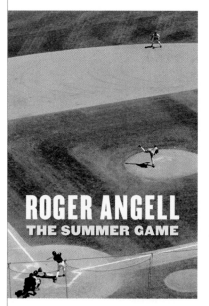

Picking Winners: A Horseplayer's Guide by Andrew Beyer. An odd choice, maybe, but how often do you find epiphany—the now-famous speed figures— and literature on the same pages? A bettor should never play the horses if he hasn't read this book because, as the Harvard-educated Beyer writes, "he is playing the toughest game in the world, one that demands a passionate, all-consuming dedication."

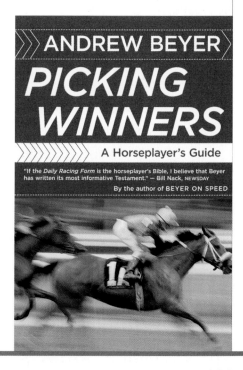

HIDING IN THE HALLS

BEHIND THE SCENES IN COOPERSTOWN AND CANTON

Fame does have its privileges. Just ask any of the recent inductees into the Baseball Hall of Fame in Cooperstown.

The baseball shrine has collected hundreds of thousands of items since opening in 1939, but it reserves some of its most historic items for a private tour that each Hall of Famer attends prior to his induction ceremonies.

The tour is designed to form a strong bond between each inductee and baseball's rich history. Steve Carlton, the first to experience the walk-through, called it a "godsend," and players have emerged with a greater understanding of baseball's impact on American culture and the way the game endures.

Newspaper articles, box scores, and artifacts, many of them dating to pre–Civil War days, are displayed on the exclusive tour. The game's newest inductees can view baseballs from the 1850s; team pictures, including an 1889 photo of Chicago's National League club on a tour of Egypt; and the earliest known player contract, signed by Levi Meyerle in February 1870 for a team in the National Association.

Baseball and politics are on display—this 1860 Currier and Ives lithograph depicts Abraham Lincoln in a victorious pose at home plate as he and his former rivals use common baseball terms to describe the just-completed presidential election.

It appears to me very singu[lar] that we three should strike "[something]" and be "put out" while old A[be] made such a "good lick".—

UNION CLUB.

FUSION.

THE NA[TIONAL]

NAL GAME. THREE "OUTS" AND ONE "RUN".
ABRAHAM WINNING THE BALL.

Equally memorable are the VIP tours at the Pro Football Hall of Fame in Canton, Ohio, created by the NFL in 2008. Suggested by former Dallas Cowboys receiver Michael Irvin to commissioner Roger Goodell in 2007, the tours are attended by all NFL draftees and rookie free agents and have a similar goal of connecting today's players to football's past. The rookies are accompanied on the tours by football Hall of Famers and Joe Horrigan, the football museum's VP of communications and exhibits.

One of the featured artifacts is known as pro football's birth certificate, a one-page accounting sheet from November 12, 1892, which indicates that William "Pudge" Heffelfinger accepted $500 to play one game of football, thus making him the first known professional.

Oakland Raiders players walk through the Pro Football Hall of Fame in Canton, Ohio, on May 28, 2008.

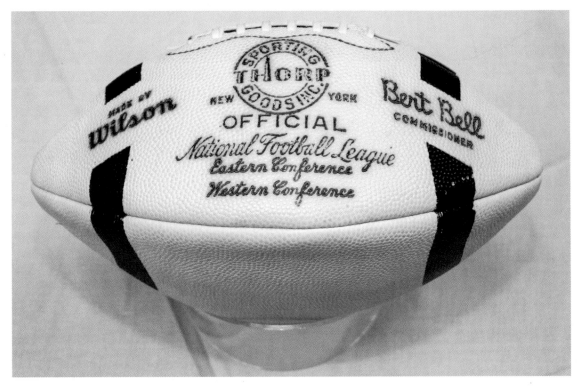

Completely white footballs like this one were used for night games in the NFL in the early 1950s.

The players get to see old leather helmets and the first face masks—invented not just to protect a player's face but also to conceal his identity during pro games so that he could continue to play as an amateur on the collegiate level. Another marvel is a white football, used for early night games, when lighting was less than ideal.

A highlight of the tour is a pair of 1946 Cleveland Browns player contracts signed by Hall of Famers Bill Willis and Marion Motley. Willis and Motley were two of the four African American players (the L.A. Rams' Kenny Washington and Woody Strode were the other two) who ended the sport's color barrier one year prior to Jackie Robinson's signing with the Brooklyn Dodgers in 1947.

Horrigan often relates stories told to him by Willis and Motley about late hits and the other forms of abuse they endured through the early years of their careers, none of which were flagged for unnecessary roughness. The impression made the first time a flag was thrown for a late hit was so vivid that Motley never forgot the name of the referee: Tommy Hughitt.

FACE VALUE

It's the final table at the 2003 World Series of Poker—top prize, $2.5 million—and the 27-year-old accountant Chris Moneymaker is playing heads up against poker professional Sam Farha. Moneymaker has nothing after the flop. Still nothing after the turn, but when Farha bets $300,000, Moneymaker raises him $500,000 on a stone-cold bluff. Farha calls. *Gulp.*

The river card is no help to Moneymaker, but he confidently pushes in all his chips and waits. And waits. Farha, who holds the winning hand, stares him down. "You must have missed your flush, huh?" he asks. No answer. After another tense minute, Farha, the pro, lays down his cards, conceding the $1.8 million pot. So yeah, Chris Moneymaker knows something about keeping a poker face.

"When he said, 'You missed your flush?' I felt it in my throat," Moneymaker recalls. "But I tried not to move a muscle. I tried to go to sleep."

That is the key to Moneymaker's poker face: He clears his mind of all thoughts. He may not literally try to fall asleep in a pressure poker situation, but he is visualizing himself on a calm beach somewhere. As anyone knows who has seen *Rounders* or watches the WSOP, poker is not about playing the cards but rather about playing your opponents. And the ability to keep a poker face—a face that lacks any interpretable expression—is the greatest skill a player can have. Of course, it's not just the face that can give away information; you must also mind your hands, feet, heart, and the rest of your body. Here are Moneymaker's tips for how not to give it up:

1. Wait until the action is yours to look at your cards. When it's your turn, take a deep breath and look at the two cards together. Players who look at their cards one at a time often pause in between if they like the first one. "They may squeeze an ace," Moneymaker says.

2. Do not be fazed by the cards you have. "In my younger days, I would get excited with pocket aces," Moneymaker says, "but I've been beat on them so many times that I know they're not a winner yet. Nothing is." Stare straight ahead and think only about how you will act in different situations.

3. If you make a bet and someone is trying to get a read on you, use visualization to remove yourself emotionally from the game. You can stare your opponent in the eyes (it's easier to actually stare at the bridge of his or her nose), or if you're not comfortable with that, you can close your eyes. You can also wear reflective sunglasses.

Chris Moneymaker at the table during the WSOP No-Limit Texas Hold'em World Championship Event in Las Vegas, Nevada, on July 31, 2006.

4. Remember, it's only a game. "You can always win and you can always lose," says Moneymaker. "Keep that in the back of your mind. I have a picture of my kids. It keeps it in perspective and makes it a lot easier."

10 COMMANDMENTS A DECALOGUE OF SPORTS SINS

Every sport has a written set of rules (law) and an unwritten set of rules (justice). Breaking the former will get you penalized. Breaking the latter will get you a fastball under the chin or a clothesline across the neck. Because codes of conduct are often lengthy, let's restrict this list to ten commandments, one per sport:

Baseball. *Thou shalt not steal with a big lead.*

Football. *Thou shalt pull your starters with a big lead in the fourth quarter.*

Hockey. *Thou shalt not give the opposing goalie a snow job.*

Golf. *Thou shalt not walk across a player's putting line.*

Tennis. *Thou shalt not use the warm-up as practice.*

Soccer. *Thou shalt kick the ball out of bounds when an opposing player gets injured.*

Auto racing. *Thou shalt not bump-draft in the turns.*

Basketball. *Thou shalt not use a full-court press with a big lead.*

Lacrosse. *Thou shalt not request an equipment check as a ploy.*

Boxing. *Thou shalt not bite off part of your opponent's ear.*

> **The longest golf course in the world is the Jade Dragon Snow Mountain Golf Club in Lijiang City, China: 8,450 yards at an elevation of 10,000 feet in the Himalayas.**

Evander Holyfield grimaces after his ear is bitten by Mike Tyson in the third round of their WBA heavyweight championship fight in Las Vegas, Nevada, on June 28, 1997.

BIG FLAP
HOW NOT TO TROT AROUND THE BASES

Perhaps the biggest sin in baseball is to call attention to yourself after hitting a home run. Yielding the round-tripper is embarrassing enough—there's no need to rub it in. Kirk Gibson pumping his fist as he rounded the bases after hitting a home run to win game 1 of the 1988 World Series—that was OK. But flipping your bat, standing at home, taking your time, or otherwise showboating in a meaningless regular-season game will invite scorn and retribution—heaped upon you or the guy coming up after you. As ESPN's Tim Kurkjian points out, "When Erubiel Durazo was new to the Diamondbacks, he took a long time rounding the bases after a home run. His teammate Matt Williams confronted him in the dugout and told him, 'That's not how we do it around here.'"

The most respectful trot belongs to the Blue Jays' Scott Rolen, who just puts his head down. Some players, though, can't help themselves. The most notorious offender was Jeffrey Leonard, a 1980s All-Star outfielder whose nicknames were Hackman and Penitentiary Face. Somewhere along the way, he came up with four different home run trots, all involving the way he held his "flaps," or arms. "One flap down" meant he would jog slowly around the bases with his inside arm straight out and angled down and his outside arm alongside his body—like an airplane banking to the left. He

hit four homers for the the Giants in the 1987 NL Championship Series to earn the series MVP honor, but his "flap down" trot was cited as the prime motivation for the victorious Cardinals.

Then there was Willie Montanez, a colorful first baseman (1966–82) who made the most of his 139 career homers. Before he got to each base, Montanez would do a little stutter step, and he would take a really big turn around first base. Recalls Tommy Hutton, a former Expos teammate who now announces for the Marlins, "He hit a home run one night off Fergie Jenkins and did his usual act. He came into the dugout and said, 'I know that SOB is going to knock me down next time.' The next time up, *boom*, Jenkins hit him. But Willie kept doing it."

Scott Rolen knows the right way to do it.

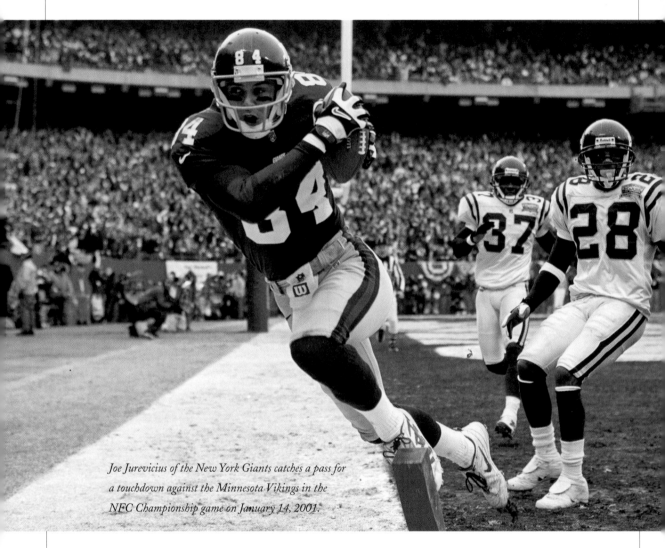

Joe Jurevicius of the New York Giants catches a pass for a touchdown against the Minnesota Vikings in the NFC Championship game on January 14, 2001.

Advertisements for new cameras often carry come-ons like "Shoot Like a Pro." Well, thanks to digital technology, action photography has become easier over the years, even for amateurs. But if you really want your photos to look professional—well, it takes more than equipment. Here, Rob Tringali, who is a photographer for *ESPN The Magazine* and has shot 19 Super Bowls, 12 World Series, and 5 Olympic Games, shares his tips.

Shooting sports requires good instincts, patience, and—this never hurts—a little luck. You can help that luck by eating right and drinking right. I can recall working a 14-inning playoff game in Fenway that lasted five hours. News flash: They aren't going to wait for you to get back from the bathroom.

You should also dress right: comfortable shoes and clothes for all occasions. I don't care if there are blue skies when you leave your house—always bring rain gear.

As for camera gear, remember that in most sporting venues, you are a good distance away from the action. So the go-to lens for most photogs is a standard 400-mm 2.8 lens. But you should also have a medium lens for action somewhere in the middle and a wide-angle for the action that ends up in your lap. Since you never know where and when the action will take place, carrying three camera bodies is a necessity.

Get to the game early; battling crowds and traffic will get you off to a bad start. Make sure your equipment is all there and working: charged batteries, flash cards, backup pieces, etc. Have a game plan for your day's assignment. What's more likely, an offensive or a defensive game? This can help out in your positioning. Look around the stadium for cool angles that no one else has sorted out yet, or cool backgrounds that would make a good photo, or maybe an interesting place to hang a camera remote for another unique look at the event. Notice your backgrounds: A security guy with a green neon jacket can ruin a great frame.

> **Bud Grant never won an NFL championship in his 18 years as a coach with the Minnesota Vikings. But he did win an NBA title as a backup forward on the 1950 Minneapolis Lakers.**

Stay alert. Just when you think the game is boring and there hasn't been a picture yet, boom—something immediately happens. And it could happen to you: Today's athletes are big and fast, and they will hurt if they hit you. Baseballs and hockey pucks travel at high speeds and can send you to the hospital—I've seen that happen quite a few times. Since you're so close to the action, all you can do to stay out of harm's way is depend on your experience. Should I keep kneeling down on the football field and get a cool frame, or should I get up and let it go? It often comes down to split-second responses. For the beginner, I would say get up and leave; for the experienced photographer, you probably know how long you can hang in there.

Remember, there are no second chances in photography. And rest assured, if you don't get the shot, one of your talented competitors will, and you'll probably see it all over the place, reminding you of how unprepared you were that day.

One last thing. You're a professional just like the athletes you're shooting. So act like one.

MIGHTIEST GAME (FOOTBALL)

HAIL MARY, FULL OF GRACE

After the game, the father of the winning quarterback said, "There'll be a million people who will say they were here for this."

On the face of it, the game should not have been a big deal: Boston College (7–2) at the University of Miami (8-3) on November 23, 1984. There was no national championship at stake; B.C. had already committed to the Cotton Bowl; the Heisman Trophy votes for Eagles quarterback Doug Flutie were already submitted.

But Flutie, the 5'9" senior, was going up against another storied QB, 6'4" sophomore Bernie Kosar, and somebody at CBS had had the prescience to move the game in the Orange Bowl, originally scheduled for September 29, to the Friday after Thanksgiving. (The network had to pay Rutgers more than $80,000 to bow out of a November 24 game with Miami.) So a lot of people with holiday time on their hands were watching.

What they saw was amazing: 15 scoring drives, none less than 55 yards; 1,273 yards of total offense, 919 of it in the air; 11 passes from Flutie to his roommate, Gerard Phelan; 92 points. Flutie threw 11 straight complete passes to start the game and stake B.C. to a 14–0 lead. Kosar rallied the Hurricanes with 11 straight completions in the second quarter. A 96-yard drive by Miami to start the second half tied the score at 28-all. Back and forth they went, toe to toe. With 3:50 remaining in the game, Flutie led an 82-yard drive that gave B.C. a 41–38 lead. Kosar took the Hurricanes right back down the field to give them a 45–41 lead.

Flutie had 80 yards to go in 28 seconds. Two complete passes and a penalty put the ball at the Miami 48 with just 6 seconds left. At this point, just as B.C. did, let's have Flutie take over:

> The last play of the game we called was 55 Flood Tip. Everybody lined up out to the right. . . . I decided I was going to drop back, try to buy some time, roll to the right, let the guys get there, and throw a jump ball. . . . I just let it heave to Gerard. . . .
>
> It's so funny to watch the tape of Gerard just chugging down the field with his head down. He didn't even bother turning around and looking until he got to the end zone. Because I was rolling right and the DBs kind of froze, he got behind them at about the 10-yard line. At the five-yard line he turned and kind of backpedaled as he saw the ball coming toward him. . . . Gerard said he tried to catch it in his stomach, but the ball slipped down and he trapped it against his thigh and fell into the end zone. When he landed he saw there was writing on the ground underneath him and knew he'd scored. Then he showed the referee he had the ball.

Officially ruled a 48-yard pass, the ball actually traveled some 65 yards in the air. As Flutie later wrote (with Perry Lefko) in his eponymous autobiography:

> The amazing thing for me was I didn't even know who caught the ball. I saw the ball fall over the heads of the two defensive backs and thought it fell incomplete. A second or two later I saw the official's arms in the back of the end zone go up and rule it a touchdown. I started shaking my head and laughing. . . . A good five minutes later, I made it to the locker room and asked our strong safety, Dave Pereira, who caught the ball. He told me Gerard did, and I kind of shook my head and said, "That figures."

Flutie may have laughed about what would become the most famous Hail Mary pass in college football history, but some people had a very different reaction. At the time of the game, Tom Coughlin was with the Philadelphia Eagles as their wide-receiver coach, but he had been Flutie's quarterback coach the year before at B.C. Here's his recollection of The Pass:

> I came home from practice and opened the door and my wife and my four children were sitting there in the family room crying, and I thought, "Oh my God, what's happened here? Has there been some kind of tragedy that I'm not aware of?" I said to my wife, "What's the matter?" She looked at me and said, "He did it again. He did it again."

Doug Flutie is held up by brother Darren after B.C.'s victory over the Miami Hurricanes.

MASKED MEN
MEET THE PATRON SAINT OF GOALIES

G iven the heft of the hard rubber puck and the speeds at which it can travel after coming off a stick, it's hard to believe that goalie masks did not come into common use until 1959. Actually, Clint Benedict of the Montreal Maroons devised a crude leather mask in 1930 after a shot by Howie Morenz of the crosstown Canadiens broke his nose, but he abandoned it after two games because it impaired his vision.

The father of the modern mask is Jacques Plante, and the birth date is November 1, 1959. That's when Plante, then with the Canadiens, was hit in the face with a shot from Andy Bathgate of the New York Rangers. Plante left the ice to get stitches and returned carrying an experimental fiberglass mask he had been using in practice. Ridiculed as a coward when he continued wearing the mask, Plante said, "If you jump from an airplane without a parachute, is that considered an act of bravery?"

Plante's mask, which resembled the one worn by Jason in the *Friday the 13th* slasher flicks, soon gave way to other innovative masks: the pretzel style worn by Ken Dryden, the Lefty Wilson models made by the assistant Detroit Red Wings trainer for Terry Sawchuk and others, hinged masks and caged masks that offered greater protection to the neck and head of the goalie. In 1976, Islanders goalie Chico Resch brought art to his mask by allowing a friend to paint it.

Today's masks bear little resemblance to Plante's pioneer model. But modern goalies still owe Plante a debt of gratitude for their well-being, not to mention their teeth. At the same time, they should lift their masks in recognition of Andy Brown. The journeyman for the Pittsburgh Penguins was the last goalie to play without a mask, on April 7, 1974. He and the Penguins lost, to the Atlanta Flames, 6–3.

> "The three important elements of hockey are: forecheck, backcheck, and paycheck."
> —former Buffalo Sabres center Gil Perreault

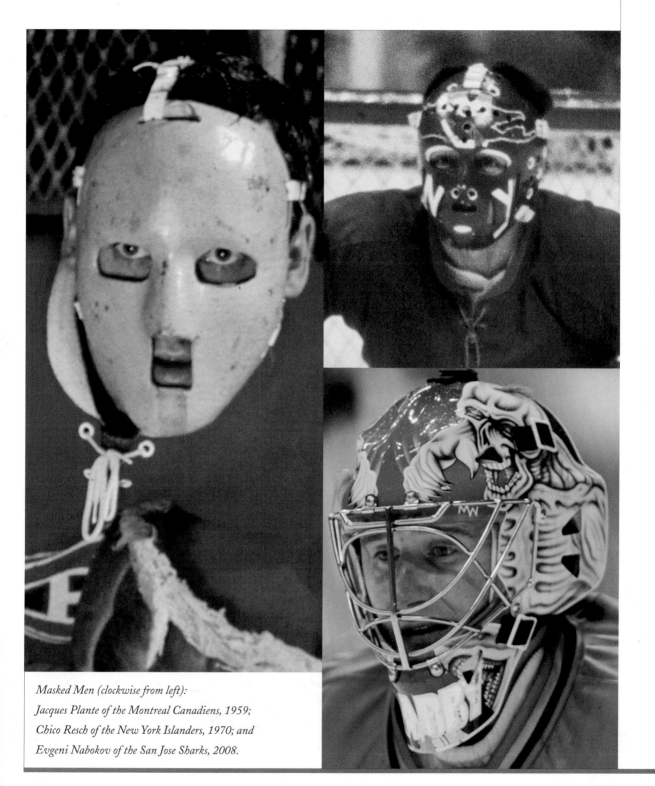

Masked Men (clockwise from left):
Jacques Plante of the Montreal Canadiens, 1959;
Chico Resch of the New York Islanders, 1970; and
Evgeni Nabokov of the San Jose Sharks, 2008.

LUCKY CHARMS ATHLETES ARE A SUPERSTITIOUS LOT

Athletes are a superstitious lot, trying to replicate success by not changing (or changing) underwear, diets, habits, schedules, routines. The fine outfielder Larry Walker, for instance, was obsessed with the number 3. His uniform was always 33, he took swings in multiples of three, he set his alarm clock for three minutes past the hour—we'll let him take it from there: "I got married in '93, on November 3 at 3:33 P.M. We were married for three years, and she got $3 million."

Below are lists of athletes and superstitions. (Though some of the players are still active, all of the superstitions are described in the past tense because, hey, the habit might have been broken.) See if you can match them up:

Bjorn Borg celebrates after winning the Wimbledon Lawn Tennis Championship, 1980.

1. Peyton Manning		A.	washed his car before every game
2. Curt Schilling		B.	spit out his gum and hit it before every AB
3. Bruce Gardiner		C.	never shaved during Wimbledon
4. Danny Ferry		D.	wore the same cup he'd worn in high school
5. Goran Ivanisevec		E.	stomped on every paper cup in the dugout
6. John Henderson		F.	sprayed his knees with WD-40
7. Kevin Millar		G.	ate a toasted PB&J 30 minutes before a game
8. Patrick Roy		H.	had trunks facing inward on all 25 elephant figures in his office
9. Mike Bibby		I.	drank a 2-liter bottle of Mountain Dew during a game
10. Lee Trevino		J.	had the trainer slap him in the face before every game
11. Nate Wayne		K.	wore a pair of black ladies' panties under his uniform
12. Billy Williams		L.	took his laces out before every game
13. Ray Bourque		M.	ate licorice, then brushed his teeth after every inning
14. Caron Butler		N.	used a Helen Hicks pitching wedge
15. Björn Borg		O.	sprinkled deer urine on his bats
16. Lawrence Tynes		P.	sprinkled his own urine on his hands before a game
17. Moises Alou		Q.	read the program cover-to-cover before every game
18. Bill Parcells		R.	underlined a book passage he liked before every game
19. Earl Weaver		S.	was always the second person up after a changeover
20. Gary Player		T.	used time-outs to clip his nails
21. Turk Wendell		U.	lit five floating candles in hotel toilets, bathtubs, and sinks
22. Brendan Donnelly		V.	dipped his stick blade in the toilet before every game
23. Rico Carty		W.	always left a ticket at the box office for his deceased father
24. Raul Mondesi		X.	talked constantly to the goalposts
25. Mark McGwire		Y.	changed balls after every birdie
26. Rob Murphy		Z.	continually wrapped and unwrapped string around his finger

Key: 1-Q, 2-W, 3-V, 4-R, 5-S, 6-J, 7-O, 8-X, 9-T, 10-N, 11-F, 12-B, 13-L, 14-I, 15-C, 16-A, 17-P, 18-H, 19-Z, 20-Y, 21-M, 22-G, 23-U, 24-E, 25-D, 26-K

"I think I was the best baseball player I ever saw."
—Willie Mays

TABLETOPS
HOW TO RULE AT
TABLE TENNIS

When you walk into the Wang Chen Table Tennis Club on the Upper West Side of Manhattan, there's no mistaking Wang's superstar status. Pictures adorning the walls feature Wang, a member of the 2008 U.S. Olympic table tennis team, with fellow U.S. Olympians LeBron James and Chris Paul, as well as with former president George H. W. Bush.

Wang, the first American to reach the quarterfinals of an Olympic table tennis tournament, is not only a world-renowned player but also a teacher of the game, offering lessons by the hour. As such, the Chinese émigré is uniquely qualified to teach the ins and outs of the most important shot in table tennis: the serve.

"We teach right-handed players to begin from the far left side of the table," says Wang, her knees slightly bent and the paddle resting softly between her thumb and index finger. She modifies her grip for the serve, placing her index finger a little lower on the back side of the paddle—"to give more wrist action."

From there, "it starts with the toss." Place the ball "right in the middle of the palm" in order to create a consistent toss of about 6 inches. As the ball descends, Wang sweeps through its left or right side, depending on whether she is hitting it with a slice spin to the opposite corner or a pull spin down the line.

The key, Wang says, is to vary your serves. "Otherwise, your opponent knows how to play you. When I play, I probably hit about 70 to 80 percent of my serves short because they're harder for the opposing player to attack."

In fact, according to Wang, there are over 30 new kinds of serves reportedly being used in tournaments around the world. The serve that all of Wang's younger students ask to learn is the traditional Chinese serve, with a very high toss. The high toss generates power from the downward force of the ball, but it has been used less and less in the professional ranks because most tournaments take place in arenas with air conditioning, which affects the flight of the ball.

Another interesting serve, Wang says, is the one employed most often by Japanese women, who, because they are shorter than many other players, can almost bend down to the height of the table and serve over their heads with a topspin.

As in any other sport, the best way to perfect your serve is practice. Wang encourages her students to experiment with their own style to find what works best for them. "Practicing serves doesn't take much energy," she says. "It's very easy and very important to winning."

For the dedicated, Wang recommends her "special secret" training trick: six spots that are worth aiming for on a serve—three along the back edge of the table (either corner and right down the middle) and those same three about a third of the way to the back of the table.

You may never make the Olympics. But with Wang's advice, the next time somebody challenges you to a friendly game of Ping-Pong, you'll be serving higher, faster, and stronger.

Wang Chen of the U.S. bears down in a preliminary-round women's singles table tennis match at the 2008 Beijing Olympic Games.

BREAKING ANKLES CHRIS PAUL ON HOW TO FAKE OUT AN OPPONENT

There may be no more thrilling play in basketball than the killer crossover. More so even than the posterizing dunk, the ankle breaker is a statement of absolute victory over a defender, a show of dominance for the victor and humiliation for the loser. Perhaps there is no one better to ask how to hone one's own ankle-breaking skill than 2008 Olympic gold medalist and NBA MVP runner-up Chris Paul of the New Orleans Hornets.

"The key is keeping the defender off-balance," says Paul. "For instance, if I'm coming up the court full speed, I may dribble real fast between my legs."

This, Paul says, gets the defender thinking about which way he wants to go.

"Then I'll go right hand to left hand to set him up."

This keeps the defender guessing.

"Then I'll dribble in and out with the left hand to get him leaning, and once I get his feet moving, I know I have him."

At that point, he crosses over from left to right, leaving the poor defender in his wake and the lane open for a layup, floater, or easy assist.

CP3, as he is affectionately called by fans, has been using his crossover as a weapon for a long time. In fact, he still remembers the moment he first knew just how dangerous his dribble was.

"My first time making someone fall down was at Walkertown [North Carolina] Middle School, when I was in eighth grade," he says. "The kid's name was Jason Jowers, and my dad was there in the stands with his video camera."

Paul says that nothing gets NBA players more excited than watching a great crossover by the likes of Jason Williams, Stephon Marbury, or—Paul's favorite—Allen Iverson.

> **Pete Maravich could dribble a basketball outside the passenger window of a car traveling 20 mph.**

Growing up, Paul emulated the crossovers of guys like Tim Hardaway. But, he says, there is no contest when it comes to naming the single best ankle breaker of all time. In fact, Paul has a special connection to him because he was a fellow Wake Forest Demon Deacon.

"No question," he says. "Randolph Childress in the 1995 ACC Tournament championship game is the best ever. Jeff McInnis of North Carolina was guarding him on the left wing. Childress had his back to him; then he turned around to go to the hoop, and he crossed over real quick, right to left, and McInnis just fell down on his back. So Childress just looks down at him, motions with his hand to tell him to get up, then hits a three—nothing but net."

As he thinks about the move, a huge smile comes across Paul's face. "Oh, man, that's all we saw when I was at Wake."

Chris Paul makes a move to the basket during a game against Greece at the 2008 Beijing Summer Olympics.

TAPING ANKLES
KEVIN CARROLL ON HOW TO WRAP AN ANKLE

Your ankle is a little balky, but you've got a big tennis match. Your child twisted an ankle, but she's got a big Pelé Cup match coming up. If you think you can gird the warrior with just any old Ace bandage, think again. And take the advice of Kevin Carroll.

As a professional trainer, Kevin Carroll has taped the ankles of Allen Iverson, Lisa Leslie, and Tiger Woods. Also the author of the inspirational *Rules of the Red Rubber Ball*, Carroll recommends consulting a licensed trainer or reading *Arnheim's Principles of Athletic Training* by William Prentice and Daniel Arnheim, before proceeding. Then follow these instructions for taping your own ankle:

1. Start by lying down with your foot facing up, in the same position it would be in if you were standing on it.

2. Begin either just above the ankle bone or at the middle of the foot, using prewrap, which you can purchase at any pharmacy. Wrap it around the foot and ankle to cover the area.

3. Take two to three strips of tape and stick them to the top of the ankle. Do the same with two to three strips at the bottom of the foot. These strips are called anchors.

4. Grab the tape and pull a piece of it lengthwise, starting from the right side of the ankle at the anchor, around the bottom of the foot and back up to the left side. Repeat this two or three times. These pieces of tape are known as stirrups.

5. Beginning at the top of the ankle, at the anchor, use seven or eight strips of tape, and place them, overlapping, toward the bottom of the ankle.

6. Continue with bigger strips, and bring the tape around the back of the heel and adhere it to the top of your foot. Do that two or three times.

7. Take the roll of tape and, starting at the instep, or inside of the foot, bring the tape along the ankle at a slight angle and wrap it around the underside of the foot and then around the outside of the heel and back around to the front. Repeat that twice, following the path you just made.

Now you're ready for battle. And now you know a little about what a professional athlete has to go through before a competition.

Erin Buescher of the Sacramento Monarchs gets taped up before Game 4 of the 2005 WNBA finals against the Connecticut Sun.

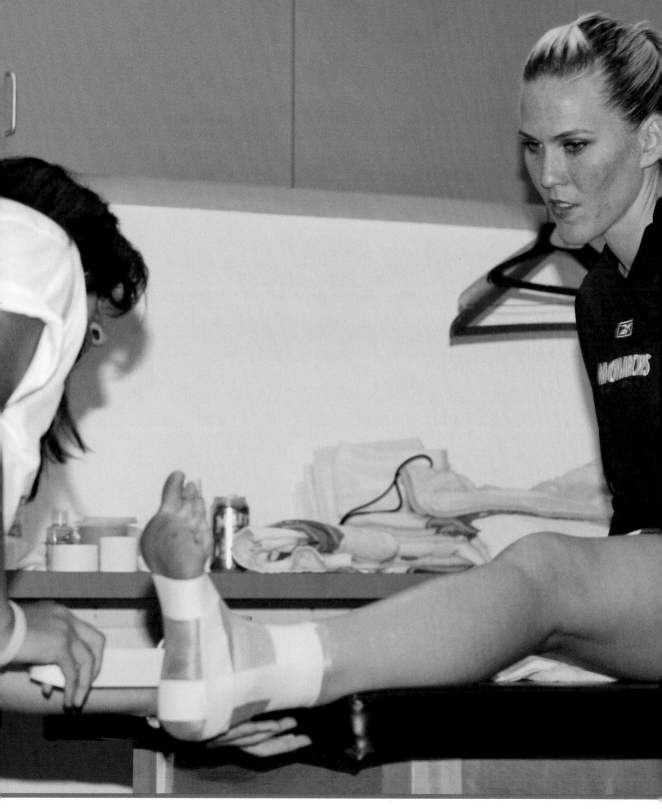

MIGHTIEST GAME (BASEBALL)
THE STORY OF THE MERKLE BONER

The national pastime has had many dramatic games over its long history, but perhaps its most memorable was also one of its most controversial: the 1908 Cubs-Giants game, in which a base-running blunder by a young Giants player negated an apparent victory and led to the Cubs' winning the 1908 National League pennant *and* their last World Series. The details could sustain a two-hour film. But here's the *Reader's Digest* version:

The Cubs (90–53) and the Giants (87–50) were in a virtual first-place tie with about two weeks left in a tight pennant race when they met at the Polo Grounds in New York on September 23. In the bottom of the 9th inning, with the score at 1–1 and Giants runners on first and third with two outs, Al Bridwell hit an apparent game-winning single to center field. But the runner on first—young Fred Merkle, playing only because of an injury to a teammate—ran off the base path toward the clubhouse, following the custom of the time, as soon as the ball hit by Bridwell reached the outfield, *without first touching second base!*

Ten years after the game, Merkle was playing with the Cubs.

The Cubs' brainy second baseman, Johnny Evers, who had unsuccessfully protested a similar play earlier in the month at Pittsburgh, called for the ball. A wrestling match ensued as the Giants' third-base coach, Iron Man McGinnity, realized what was happening and struggled with Evers for the ball. Some say the ball was thrown over the stadium roof, but Evers eventually produced *a* ball, stood on second base, and appealed to umpire Hank O'Day for an out call. By chance, O'Day had been the umpire for the earlier game at Pittsburgh, and although he had ruled against Evers that day, he'd later told Evers that upon reflection he'd realized that the second baseman was correct and that a force-out on a runner from first base should negate the apparent winning run. So O'Day called Merkle out.

> **"Anybody with ability can play in the big leagues. But to be able to trick people year in and year out the way I did, I think that was a much greater feat."**
> —broadcaster and former major league catcher Bob Uecker

Now, with thousands of fans on the field and further play impossible, each team claimed victory: The Giants said they had won 2–1, while the Cubs claimed a forfeit win because the marauding fans would not allow the game to resume. The umpires called the game a tie, and both teams protested to the league president. Giants manager John McGraw was especially livid, believing that a bona fide victory had been stolen. Legend has it that he even brought Merkle and Christy Mathewson back to a darkened Polo Grounds just before midnight and had Mathewson witness Merkle stepping onto second base so that Mathewson—the most universally respected player in baseball at the time—could assert that he saw Merkle touch the base that day.

But National League president Harry Pulliam upheld the ruling of a tie, with the game to be replayed at the end of the season only if it became necessary to determine the pennant winner. Of course, it came to exactly that. Each team stood at 98–55 when the Cubs returned to New York for the replay on October 8. Mordecai "Three-Finger" Brown, pitching in relief for the Cubs, defeated Mathewson 4–2, and the Cubs won the pennant.

If this were a movie, these are the postscripts that would appear:

The Cubs downed the Tigers in the 1908 World Series but haven't won another series since.

Merkle played in 16 seasons in the majors, batting .273 and participating in five World Series, but never lived down the nickname Bonehead.

Pulliam, who lived and worked in New York, became the subject of a constant stream of abuse from the Giants and their fans. In July of 1909, he killed himself.

MISSPELL CHECK

IT PAYS TO MAKE A MISTAKE— ON BASEBALL CARDS

red Merkle may never have cashed in, but there's real money in mistakes. Take the baseball-card business, for instance. The most expensive card in the world is the 1909 T-206 Honus Wagner, one of which recently sold for $2.8 million. But the Sherry Magie card from that same American Tobacco Company set is also worth a windfall. That's because the Phillies outfielder's name was actually spelled Magee, and the manufacturers corrected the mistake during production. According to Grant Sandground, a senior analyst for *Graded Card Investor*, "A correct version is worth about $40. But a card spelled Magie, even in poor condition, is worth about $10,000. It's darn rare."

Certain baseball cards in almost-pristine condition are worth surprisingly more than others bearing the image of more famous players. Says Sandground, "Some of the values for seemingly commonplace cards that have 'low population data' can soar in value past the superstars in the same set." A case in point is the 1962 Topps Frank Robinson. A 10-point scale is used to measure the condition of a card, and collectors try to complete sets with a grade of 8 or higher. When the Robinson cards were printed, many had poorly centered borders. So an 8–10 Robinson with

centered borders is worth about $1,800, $300 more than a Mickey Mantle card in the same condition.

Here are three other cards that benefited from errors:

1987 Donruss Barry Bonds from Opening-Day Boxed Set. In a set produced for toy stores in the United States, Donruss printed a card with Barry Bonds's name but a picture of one of his teammates, Pirates second baseman Johnny Ray. Value: $250.

1990 Topps Frank Thomas. On certain versions of this card, the Big Hurt's name is missing due to the use of the wrong ink. Value: $500–$600.

2006 Topps Alex Gordon. The Royals third baseman wasn't supposed to appear in the set because he was still in the minor leagues. The MLB Players Association asked Topps to stop the print run after collectors found the card. Value: $400.

OPPOSITE PAGE:

A baseball fan digs through the offerings at the Baseball Card and Autograph Show in New York City.

MAGEE, PHILA. NAT'L

CARD GAMES HOW TO PLAY WITH MAJOR LEAGUERS

Back before collecting became a business, baseball cards were actually worth a lot more. Instead of hermetically sealing them as futures, children of the fifties and sixties used them to while away recesses, soup up bikes, and throw down gauntlets. Instead of keeping a 1962 Frank Robinson under lock and key, we were much more likely to put him up against the wall of P.S. 16 and try to knock him down.

The game was called knocksies. Here are the basic rules, along with some of the other ways we made pieces of cardboard come to life:

Knocksies. Pretty simple. We leaned three to five well-worn cards against a wall and flipped other cards to try to knock them down. Winner took all. We wanted to put a little curve in the flight because a dead-on hit often bounced off.

Topsies. We kept throwing cards until one landed on another. Again, winner took all. The bigger the venue, the better, because it increased the size of the pot. Many an argument erupted over whether one card was on top of another or just touching.

Farsies. The most macho of games—who could flip a card the farthest. We had to be willing to bet a certain number of cards on the outcome—say, 10. It's amazing how some skills never leave you. I just threw a 1983 Buck Martinez 15 feet.

Golf. Long before Frisbee golf, we had card golf. We'd set up an 18-hat layout throughout one of our houses, the object being to flip a card into each hat in the fewest number of tries. It was kind of Arnold Palmer meets Arnold Earley.

Spokespeople. You never hear the sound anymore: *thwap, thwap, thwap, thwapthwapthwap. THWAPTHWAPTHWAP.* We created it by affixing a baseball card to one of the forks on our bicycle wheel with a clothespin (another antique). The faster we went, the louder the *thwap*. We were pretty much sacrificing the life of the baseball card, but that's what quadruples of Bubba Phillips were for.

> "Baseball is the only thing beside the paper clip that hasn't changed."
> —Bill Veeck Jr.

On August 21, 1908, Washington Senators catcher Gabby Street became the first person to catch a ball dropped from the top of the Washington Monument (555 feet)— after missing the first 12.

TAKE 2 ERROR-DIRECTOR: FIVE SPORTS-MOVIE ERRORS

Sports movies have the ability to uplift and inspire. They also frequently baffle and deceive. In trying to evoke feelings of hope and triumph in their audiences, filmmakers and actors may take liberties that leave the keenest viewers scratching their heads. For those of you who are bewildered by the way that final play lasted 45 seconds when there were only 4.1 left on the clock, here are the five biggest sports-movie blunders:

Rudy (1993). In the scene that takes place right before the big game (the game Rudy plays in), the stadium shows the Penn State Blue Band on the field playing the Penn State fight song. Some may consider this odd, since Notre Dame is playing Georgia Tech.

Field of Dreams (1989). "Shoeless" Joe Jackson was known for a lot of things. One of them was batting left-handed. However, Ray Liotta portrays him as a righty, belting homers into left (corn)field.

Hoosiers (1986). During Hickory High's first practice under Coach Norman Dale, two of the seven Hoosiers quit the team. One of those players, Whit, reluctantly returns, bringing the grand total to six. The seventh member, Buddy, is never shown rejoining the team, yet halfway through the film we start seeing him again in the games and on the bench. Columnist Bill Simmons was particularly tormented by this when he wrote in 2002: "Was the 'Buddy returns and asks forgiveness' scene simply cut from the movie? Was it ever written in the first place? Did the director think that we wouldn't notice that a seven-man roster inexplicably went back to eight? This one's been bothering me for 16 years."

D2: The Mighty Ducks (1994). To begin the shootout in the championship against Iceland, the Ducks call on Jesse Hall (played by Brandon Quintin Adams) to take the first shot. Hall might've been one of the Ducks' best players, but it is still hard to believe that he could switch from playing left-handed to playing right-handed midshot. He is holding the stick as a lefty when he starts the penalty shot, switches to righty when driving to the net, and then scores a beautiful goal left-handed. It is an almost believable feat until you realize that . . .

The Sandlot (1993). DeNunez is also played by Brandon Quintin Adams. When he pitches to Ham (Patrick Renna), he says he is going to throw him the heater. The pitch is actually high and outside. And Ham pops it up—only it goes over the fence for a home run. As Ham rounds the bases, he announces, "Low and outside, just like I like it." The pitch was clearly high and out of the strike zone, proving that when Brandon Quintin Adams is involved, a sports-movie blunder can't be far away.

Brandon Quintin Adams (far right) and the gang in The Sandlot.

LEADING LADIES THE WOMAN BEHIND TITLE IX

We now know it as Title IX, and we certainly know its impact on gender equity. Since its passage as part of the Education Amendments of 1972, female participation in sports has risen by 904 percent in high school and 456 percent in college.

After the death of one of the authors of the bill, Congresswoman Patsy T. Mink, in 2002, Title IX was renamed the Patsy T. Mink Equal Opportunity in Education Act. While the representative from Hawaii did play a significant role, the primary heroine of Title IX's passage has gone largely unrecognized.

She was Edith Green, a former teacher who served as the representative from Oregon's Third Congressional District from 1955 to 1974. Known variously as Mrs. Education and the Wicked Witch of the West, she was an acknowledged expert on higher education. As recounted in *Let Me Play,* Karen Blumenthal's book on Title IX, Green proposed adding a little section to the omnibus education bill that the House Education and Labor Committee was crafting in 1972. Called Title X until another item fell away, the section banned gender discrimination in programs and activities at schools receiving federal money. Some committee members dismissed Green's addition as frivolous, but it was approved nonetheless.

> **LPGA golfer Beth Daniel birdied nine holes in a row on her way to a round of 62 at the 1999 Philips Invitational.**

The next obstacle was passage by the House. Because the bill dealt with other controversial issues, like school busing, Green hoped that Title IX would go unnoticed. She even advised women's rights activists to remain silent on the subject. Although Title IX was altered to some extent in the House, its guiding principle remained intact.

Ironically, the education bill that went before both houses of Congress was so altered in conference committees that Green ended up voting against it. But the bill passed anyway, going into effect in June of 1973. A few months later, it dawned on some members of the NCAA that the unequal distribution of resources for

Edith Green and Senator John F. Kennedy at a memorial dinner, 1959.

men's and women's sports—the University of Michigan had a budget of $2.6 million for men's sports but $0 for women's— might now be illegal.

The rest is history. And equality. Green passed away in 1987, having realized, as she said in 1978, that "every young girl [now knows] that there is no ceiling of expectations, . . . no height to which she cannot go." There should be a statue honoring her somewhere—or at every female sporting event.

> **Joan Payson, the original owner of the New York Mets, wanted to name them the Meadowlarks.**

SIT FOR THE GOLD

Casual observers of the Olympics might think that the easiest way to get a gold medal is to serve as the coxswain on a very good rowing team. All you really have to do is sit and yell and be small, right? Wrong.

The coxswain, who sits in the stern, has to keep the crew safe, steer the boat straight, and use the right words and cadence to push the rowers' buttons all the way to the finish line ahead of everyone else. The job is much more involved than it looks. Let's have Mary Whipple, the University of Washington grad who coxed the U.S. women's eight 2,000 meters to gold in the Beijing Olympics, put us through the paces:

The most important thing a coxswain does day to day is command the boat and everyone's safety. If the coach uses us right, it's a brilliant concept. During practice, he's telling me, and then I'm telling the girls, what to do. If it doesn't come from me, it can get very chaotic.

In a race, if things are going well, I don't talk at all about technique. I tell them where we are, when we want to focus a little bit more on a certain aspect, like if we want to make a move, if we want to capitalize on a little bit more speed in a certain part of a race.

You don't even think about steering in a race because we just go so hard and constant. I'm just clamping onto that gunwale, just pulling the rudder taut, making sure I don't move it out of nerves or anything. A lot of coxswains just move and jiggle the rudder out of boredom or just out of not concentrating. I steer pretty well. After safety, steering is the number one job.

I'm very aware of my surroundings. I think that's what makes me a good coxswain. I have a lot of good peripheral vision, and I can see scenarios kind of unfold, and then I have a plan.

I first got the position on the national team in 2001. The rowers vote, so our coach at the time said, "When thinking about choosing a coxswain, I have three criteria that I want you to base your decision on. The first one is, Do they steer straight? The second one: They *must* steer straight. And the third one is they *better* steer straight." And I heard that. It was like, Zip the lip and steer straight. A lot of the time when coxswains give instruction, they don't notice where they are, and they don't hold their line. And rowers can see where you go; you leave a little track. If they see all these wiggles, it just gets frustrating for them.

I guess what makes me the best is that I know when not to talk and when to let the momentum of the rowing dictate what I say. It's also how to deliver a scenario positively if we're

behind. For instance, there was one race in Lucerne before the Olympics, and we went off the line, and I'm looking around and we're fifth out of six off the start. However, the team that was leading was only two seats ahead of us. So I just said, "We're in the pack; we're two seats from the lead." And then everyone's like, "Ah, sweet, we're right there." If I had said, "We're fifth," everyone would have been freaked out and maybe a little bit tight and tense and would have tried moving the boat individually. We won because we made sure we got down to our race rhythm and just maximized our base cadence.

Coxswain Mary Whipple (front row, far right) and the U.S. women's eight.

You have to be honest, but you also have to be very positive. I have a lot of faith in my girls. For example, at the Olympics, during our third 500, when the field normally likes to close in on us, our number one goal was Don't slow down. I kept looking over to Romania, who was in second, and they never moved on us. I just kept telling the rowers, "They're still there." Not in a "keep going, keep going" way, just like, "We're holding them." And then a couple more strokes and "We're still holding them." And then the third time I said it, I was like, "We're *holding* them."

When we crossed that line, it was pure satisfaction, just simple elation. You just feel on top of the world.

PAPER PIGSKIN

In the vast expanse that is the landscape of sports, one game stands above all others for its rebellious rejection of authority. Students play the game to the chagrin of their teachers, employees face off when their bosses aren't looking, and kids carry on through the nagging of parents warning them to clean up their mess—and all it takes is the flick of a finger and a digital goal post. The game, of course, is paper football.

Those looking to steal a few moments of fun here or there are more inclined to simply attempt field goals against each other. One player makes an upright by touching his thumbs together and extending his index fingers skyward, while the opponent rests the paper football on some surface and tries to flick it through the goal posts, generally using the index finger.

The more involved paper football game is played on a tabletop surface, and begins with the paper football lying flat on the table while two players sit across from each other. The two players then push or flick the ball toward each other's edge of the table. If the ball hangs over the edge without falling over, it is a touchdown, with an extra point attempt to follow. A player attempts a field goal if his opponent flicks the ball out of bounds off the side of the table.

Making a paper football is like eating a Reese's peanut butter cup—there's no wrong way to do it. But in the interests of high-scoring games and long-distance "kicks," what follow are the directions to create the most aerodynamic paper football:

First things first: find a piece of paper. Any kind will do, although computer sheets and looseleaf generally make the best paper pigskin. While the first step is often the vertical fold, that often creates a slightly bulkier ball. That's why the best first course of action is to cut the piece of paper in half vertically, as precisely as possible.

Once you have the half piece, the next step is another exact vertical fold down the middle. Make sure your paper is folded as tightly as possible. From here, the triangle folding begins.

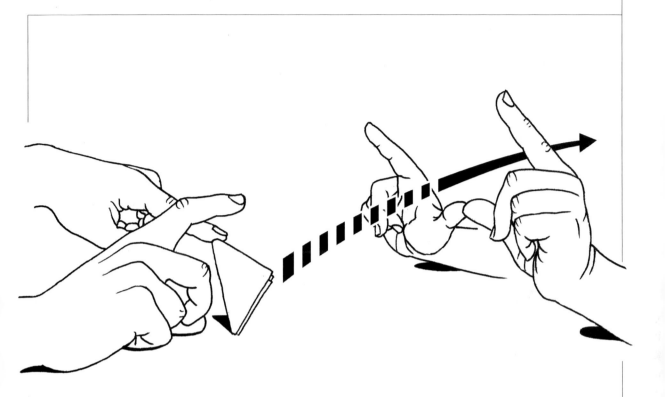

Take one of the top corners of the half page and delicately fold it down to form what should become a perfect triangle. Then continue folding that triangle down the page, stopping along the way to make sure there is as little slack as possible. The tighter the paper, the better it will fly.

After around seven folds, you will be left with a small rectangle at the bottom of the page; this is where the piece of paper becomes the game ball. Take the rectangle and fold it into the opening in the triangle located right above it. Again, the tighter the fold inside, the more distance and height you'll be able to create.

Now you should be left with the perfect paper football to flick through the uprights. (Brown coloring and faux laces are optional.) Just try not to get caught.

FALL CLASSICS YOGI BERRA'S FIVE FAVORITE WORLD SERIES GAMES

Lawrence Peter Berra played in a record 75 World Series games (all with the Yankees) from 1947 to 1963. Here, Yogi lists his five favorite Series games:

Game 5, 1956 World Series, vs. the Dodgers. "Everybody knows about this one. Don Larsen pitched his perfect game. I was behind the plate. It had never happened before, and it hasn't happened since."

When asked where he wanted to be buried, Yogi Berra said, "Surprise me."

OPPOSITE PAGE:

Yankee pitcher Don Larsen wraps his arms around catcher Yogi Berra (number 8) after the final pitch of Game 5 of the 1956 World Series against the Brooklyn Dodgers at Yankee Stadium in New York.

Game 7, 1956 World Series, vs. the Dodgers. "Everyone forgets about this game because of the perfect game. Johnny Kucks pitched a three-hit shutout, and he didn't even know he was going to pitch that day. We won 9–nothing, and I hit two two-run home runs. I hit .429 for the Series, too. I should have gotten the car [MVP], but Larsen had to get it."

Game 4, 1950 World Series, vs. the Phillies. "We swept the Phillies in '50. They only scored seven runs in the Series. It was Whitey Ford's rookie year, and he threw eight shutout innings. Then in the 9th, Gene Woodling mishandled a ball in left field, and they scored two runs. Casey took Whitey out, and the fans were booing like crazy. But Allie Reynolds came in and got the final out. Nineteen fifty was probably my best year. I hit .322 and had 124 RBIs. But the little guy, Phil Rizzuto, beat me out for the MVP. He hit .324."

Game 7, 1952 World Series, vs. the Dodgers. "Bob Kuzava, a journey-man lefty, came in to pitch in the 7th inning. The Dodgers loaded the bases, and Casey left him in to pitch to Jackie Robinson. Jackie hit this windblown pop-up near the mound that everybody lost in the sun. We froze. Everybody but Billy Martin. He came running in like crazy from second base and made the catch. Kuzava finished the game, and we won 4–2."

Game 1, 1949 World Series, vs. the Dodgers. "This was the begin-ning of the dynasty, and it was the first World Series shown on national TV. Allie Reynolds went nine innings and beat Don Newcombe in a 1–nothing shutout. Tommy Henrich was 36 years old and in his last year as a regular with the Yankees. He hit a solo home run in the bottom of the 9th inning to win the game. It was the first walk-off home run in World Series history."

THE REAL GIPPER THE MAN WHO INSPIRED THE FAMOUS SPEECH

This is Pat O'Brien as Knute Rockne speaking from his wheelchair to rally his underdog Notre Dame players after the scoreless first half of their 1928 game in Yankee Stadium against undefeated Army in the 1940 movie *Knute Rockne, All-American:*

I'm going to tell you something I've kept to myself for years. None of you ever knew George Gipp. It was long before your time.

But you know what a tradition he is at Notre Dame. . . . And the last thing he said to me—

"Rock," he said, "sometime, when the team is up against it, and the breaks are beating the boys, tell them to go out there with all they got and win just one for the Gipper. I don't know where I'll be then, Rock," he said. "But I'll know about it—and I'll be happy."

The players throw off their blankets and go out to beat Army, 12–6.

In that movie, Ronald Reagan played George Gipp, who is still considered the greatest athlete in Notre Dame history. But if you know the Gipper just from that movie, you're missing something. In fact, his life would make a more interesting movie than the one we all know.

Born in Laurium, on Michigan's Upper Peninsula, in 1895, Gipp didn't arrive on the South Bend campus until he was 21. He had won a baseball scholarship, but in the spring of his freshman year, he ignored the coach's bunt sign and hit a home run. When the coach asked him, "Don't you remember the signals?" Gipp replied, "It's too hot to be running around the bases after a bunt." He quit the team the next day.

His football prowess was already apparent, though: He drop-kicked a 62-yard field goal as a freshman. He nearly punted his academic career as well, spending much of his free time in pool halls and gambling establishments and cutting so many classes that he was asked to leave the school in 1919. But the Fighting Irish alumni intervened; Gipp was readmitted to the school and reinstated on the team. He practiced when he chose, but nobody complained—he was that good.

In the 1920 season, down 17–14 at the half to Army, Rockne was in the middle of one of his speeches when he noticed that Gipp looked bored. Rockne said to Gipp, "I don't suppose you have any interest in this game?" And Gipp replied, "Don't worry, I have $500 on it, and I don't intend to blow my money." Gipp ended up rushing for 385 yards and running a kickoff back for a touchdown as Notre Dame won 27–17.

Two weeks later, Gipp dislocated a shoulder, and Notre Dame fell behind 10–0, but in the fourth quarter the star ignored Rockne's attempts to keep him on the bench, running for one touchdown and turning himself into a decoy for the game winner. After that game, Gipp went off to Chicago to teach a prep school team how to kick, and the miserable conditions there brought on a fever and sore throat. Gipp stayed on the bench for most of the next game, against Northwestern, but the fans wanted him, and Rockne acceded, allowing Gipp to throw a 55-yard touchdown pass.

By Thanksgiving, though, Gipp was in the hospital with strep throat and pneumonia. On December 14, he converted to Catholicism and was given the last rites. The entire student body knelt in the snow on campus to pray for him. As he lay sleeping in his hospital bed, someone said, "It's tough to go." Gipp heard it and said, "What's tough about it?"

There are those who doubt the truth of Rockne's account, that Gipp turned to his coach on his deathbed and said, "I've got to go, Rock. It's all right. Sometime, when the team is up against it . . ."

But it made for a great story, not to mention a stirring halftime speech. And it helped keep the legend of George Gipp alive.

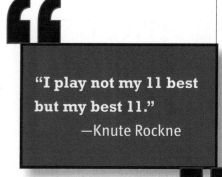

"I play not my 11 best but my best 11."
—Knute Rockne

HORSES CALLED MEN

THOROUGHBREDS NAMED AFTER FAMOUS PEOPLE

Thoroughbred owners must submit proposed names for their horses to the Jockey Club, the governing body of the sport of kings since 1894. According to registrar Rick Bailey, there are some 450,000 names in his database, all of which adhere to these essential rules:

1. The name must pass a phonetic check, meaning that it can't even sound like another registered name. (C Biskit sounds like Seabiscuit.)
2. The name can't be longer than 18 characters.
3. No obscene names are allowed. (True story: Years ago, a Florida sportswriter was given two weeks' notice and made to work on the agate pages. He spent much of his remaining time renaming horses to make them offensive. When finally caught, he said, "What are you going to do, fire me?")
4. No personal names, unless permission is received. And it sometimes is. Below is a list of thoroughbreds with famous names:

Horse	Inspiration
Chris Evert	tennis player
Oscar Schindler	Oskar Schindler, the German entrepreneur and humanitarian
Howie Long	NFL Hall of Fame DE
Jaklin Klugman	his co-owner, the actor Jack Klugman
Herschelwalker	Herschel Walker, NFL RB
Willard Scott	weatherman
Brian Boitano	ice-skater
Ann Landers	advice columnist
Joe Namath	NFL QB
Mickey Rooney	actor
Fred Astaire	actor-dancer
Rickover	Admiral Hyman G. Rickover
Leo Castelli	art dealer
Barbara Bush	First Lady

Horse	Inspiration
Nijinsky and Nijinsky II	ballet great Vaslav Nijinsky
Jimmy Stewart	actor
Frank Deford	sportswriter
Shecky Greene	comedian

Shecky Greene the man (left) and Shecky Greene the horse (right).

"It's more difficult getting up early in the morning when you're wearing silk pajamas."
—Hall of Fame jockey Eddie Arcaro

GETTING NOTICED
HOW TO SHINE AT A TRYOUT

Jeff Bradley is a senior writer for *ESPN The Magazine* and the father of two preteen boys who travel all over New Jersey to compete in baseball, soccer, cross-country, and golf. Jeff also happens to be the younger brother of Bob Bradley, coach of the U.S. men's national soccer team, and Scott Bradley, a former major league catcher who has coached baseball at Princeton University since 1998. When it comes to athletic advice for his two boys, Jeff is not shy about asking his brothers for their input. Here are their responses to the question "What's the best way for a player to get noticed at a tryout?"

1. Show your best attribute.

Scott: "Being average across the board is probably not going to get you noticed at a tryout with a lot of players, so it's important that if you have one special tool—a good arm or foot speed, for example—make sure to put it on display. One great asset is more likely to get you recognized than five midlevel skills."

2. Don't let attitude be a question.

Bob: "Dress to play, including the right footwear for multiple surfaces, because you never know when weather or the availability of facilities can force a tryout to a different venue. The player who comes prepared for every set of conditions will make a good impression."

3. Hustle, but don't go crazy.

Scott: "Run on and off the field for sure, but don't feel the need to dive for balls that are clearly out of reach, or to sprint everywhere, unless a coach orders it. Being a slug will get you bad marks for sure, but going over the top can also make a coach think your hustle is for show."

4. Don't forget that beauty is in the eye of the beholder.

Bob: "When a coach is trying to evaluate a large number of players, he's not going to see everything, and he's going to make some decisions that are wrong. So coming up short at a tryout does not mean you're a bad player. At the next tryout, you could be the player getting recognized while another good player gets overlooked."

SLIM AND NONE
YOUR CHANCES OF BECOMING A PRO

Now that we've told you what a coach might be looking for in a tryout, we have to tell you something else you may not want to hear: the chances of an athlete's getting paid to play a sport, whether with a college scholarship or a salary. Here, thanks to Tom Farrey's excellent book on youth sports, *Game On,* is a chart outlining the odds of a high school athlete's playing his or her high school sport in college:

Sport	Number of Division I Teams	Odds of Making a Division I Team	Total Number of Teams	Odds of Making Any School's Team
MEN				
Rowing	24	1 in 2	59	1 in 1
Fencing	21	1 in 5	36	1 in 3
Gymnastics	17	1 in 8	19	1 in 7
Rifle	22	1 in 15	35	1 in 9
Ice hockey	58	1 in 22	133	1 in 9
Lacrosse	56	1 in 28	214	1 in 9
Swimming and diving	141	1 in 30	381	1 in 14
Water polo	21	1 in 33	46	1 in 18
Football	234	1 in 42	614	1 in 18
Skiing	14	1 in 47	35	1 in 21
Baseball	286	1 in 48	873	1 in 17
Cross-country	299	1 in 48	865	1 in 18
Golf	289	1 in 53	762	1 in 20
Track and field	261	1 in 56	656	1 in 24
Tennis	265	1 in 59	742	1 in 21
Soccer	197	1 in 67	737	1 in 19
Wrestling	86	1 in 100	224	1 in 42
Basketball	326	1 in 111	1,000	1 in 35
Volleyball	22	1 in 111	79	1 in 37

> **Ken Rosewall can claim to be both the youngest (18 years, 2 months in 1953) and oldest (37 years, 2 months in 1972) Australian Open men's champion.**

Sport	Number of Division I Teams	Odds of Making a Division I Team	Total Number of Teams	Odds of Making Any School's Team
WOMEN				
Rowing	85	2 in 1*	141	3 in 1
Equestrian	13	1 in 2	39	1 in 1
Fencing	27	1 in 4	45	1 in 2
Rifle	27	1 in 4	36	1 in 4
Ice hockey	29	1 in 11	74	1 in 4
Gymnastics	63	1 in 16	85	1 in 12
Lacrosse	80	1 in 26	264	1 in 9
Water polo	31	1 in 26	61	1 in 15
Swimming and diving	188	1 in 30	489	1 in 14
Golf	228	1 in 31	483	1 in 16
Cross-country	321	1 in 33	940	1 in 14
Field hockey	77	1 in 37	257	1 in 11
Skiing	16	1 in 39	39	1 in 19
Soccer	301	1 in 42	913	1 in 15
Track and field	295	1 in 42	704	1 in 22
Tennis	309	1 in 62	876	1 in 20
Softball	264	1 in 72	911	1 in 23
Bowling	28	1 in 83	45	1 in 50
Volleyball	311	1 in 91	982	1 in 29
Basketball	323	1 in 100	1,025	1 in 31

If those numbers are not sobering enough, consider that a person's odds of winning an Olympic medal are 662,000 to 1, slightly longer than the odds of getting hit by lightning (576,000 to 1), and that the odds of becoming a pro athlete are 22,000 to 1, making it about twice as hard as winning an Academy Award (11,500 to 1).

But fame and fortune should never be the reasons for playing sports. The skills acquired from self-improvement, the camaraderie of being part of a team, the health benefits from exercise, the lessons that will last a lifetime—those are the reasons.

*As a sport, rowing is a statistical anomaly. Colleges tend to have large women's teams, in part to offset large rosters of football players on the men's side. As a result, there are more women on NCAA-sponsored crew teams than there are on high school squads.

"The time when there is no one there to feel sorry for you or to cheer for you is when a player is made."
—Tim Duncan

THROWS LIKE A GIRL

THE WOMAN WHO STRUCK OUT RUTH AND GEHRIG

At the 2003 All-Star Game at Comiskey Park in Chicago, softball star Jennie Finch pitched against a gauntlet of major leaguers—Mike Piazza, Albert Pujols, Mike Cameron, Paul Lo Duca—and struck them all out with a softball thrown from 43 feet away. As impressive as her feat was, it pales in comparison with one performed by a 17-year-old girl 72 years earlier.

The girl was Jackie Mitchell, and she grew up in Memphis, next door to a future Hall of Famer, Dazzy Vance. Vance noticed her talent and taught her to throw his favorite pitch, a curveball that dropped off the table. In 1931, while attending a baseball school in Atlanta, the 17-year-old came to the attention of Joe Engel, the owner of the Chattanooga Lookouts. He offered her a contract to play for the Lookouts, which she signed on March 28.

As it happens, the New York Yankees were traveling north from spring training in Florida, and on April 2 the Bronx Bombers stopped in Chattanooga to play an exhibition game. A crowd of 4,000 showed up. Lookouts starting pitcher Clyde Barfoot gave up a double to Earle Combs and a single to Lyn Lary, at which point manager Bert Niehoff brought in the left-handed Mitchell to face none other than Babe Ruth.

Dressed in a baggy uniform custom-made for her by Spalding, Mitchell missed high with her first pitch. But Ruth swung at and missed her second pitch. And her third pitch. He let the fourth go by, but it caught the corner of the plate for strike 3. According to accounts, Ruth "kicked the dirt, called the umpire a few dirty names, gave his bat a wild heave, and stomped out to the Yanks' dugout."

Quite possibly, Ruth was putting on a show. But the next batter, Lou Gehrig, swung at and missed three pitches. After a standing ovation that lasted several minutes, Mitchell walked Tony Lazzeri. At that point, Niehoff replaced her with Barfoot.

A few days after Mitchell had struck out two of the greatest players of all time, commissioner Kenesaw Mountain Landis voided her contract and declared women

"**The only change is that baseball has turned Paige from a second-class citizen to a second-class immortal.**"
—Negro Leagues great Satchel Paige

unfit to play baseball. Mitchell continued to play for the barnstorming House of David team, but she retired from baseball altogether at the age of 23, preferring to work for her father, an eye doctor.

It was kind of ironic, her helping the shortsighted.

Lou Gehrig and Babe Ruth watch female pitching phenom Jackie Mitchell demonstrate her fastball in Chattanooga, Tennessee, in 1931.

CREATURE FEATURE THE ORIGINAL PHANATIC'S BEST AND WORST

When it comes to mascot knowledge, **Dave Raymond** is the veritable wrangler of all things fuzzy and neon green. The original Phillie Phanatic, Raymond is now the "Emperor of Fun and Games" (translation: CEO) of Raymond Entertainment Group, a company that designs mascots and advises teams on the marketability of turquoise fur. Here are his lists of five best and five worst mascots:

The Best

The San Diego Chicken. "He is the first mascot to truly entertain," Raymond says of Ted Giannoulas, the original chicken. Introduced in 1974 by a radio station to distribute Easter eggs at the San Diego Zoo, the Chicken became a fixture at Padre games and landed on *The Sporting News* list of top 100 people in sports in the twentieth century. He was once sued by the producers of Barney the dinosaur for beating up a look-alike.

The Phillie Phanatic. "Totally unexpected," says Raymond of the Phanatic's success. "There's a backstory to what made the Phanatic a phenomenon. The Phillies' brass did not try to shove the Phanatic down the fans' throats. They let the mascot grow naturally, by encouraging him to entertain the players as well as the fans. That broke down the barrier that exists between fans and athletes and showed that those who competed on the field were human."

Go, the Phoenix Gorilla. Says Raymond, "He is the best physical performer of all professional mascots." Whether jumping through rings of fire or kibitzing with fans, Go has become one of the Phoenix Suns' biggest draws. And as Raymond says, "Honestly, who would ever imagine a gorilla in Phoenix?"

Clutch, the Houston Rockets Bear. Raymond presented Clutch with the NBA's inaugural Mascot of the Year award in 2005. Clutch has height (at 6-foot-8) and hops, and he shares a pedigree with the Phanatic: Both Raymond and Bob Boudwin, the original Clutch, are graduates of the University of Delaware.

Rocky, the Denver Nuggets Mountain Lion. According to Raymond, "The NBA is the best league for mascots because they believe in the value of character development. It is the only league that gives awards to top performers and treats them as a valuable addition to game operations."

178   CREATURE FEATURE

The Worst

The San Francisco Giants' Crazy Crab. Bad mascots are indictments of teams that do not see value in fan entertainment. Topping the list is the anti-mascot, the Crab, who debuted in 1984 to embody all the complaints about Candlestick Park. "The fans hated it so much they pelted it with veggies every time it came out," says Raymond. Manager Frank Robinson attacked the Crab in a local commercial spot, but the Crab made a bobblehead comeback in 2008.

Izzy. The official mascot of the 1996 Summer Olympics in Atlanta, Izzy was derided as "blue sperm" by the media. Says Raymond, "It was originally called Whatizit after it was unveiled in 1992. Nobody knew what it was then or now, and neither did the Olympic Committee."

The Pittsburgh Steelers' Steely McBeam. Raymond points out that despite the mascot's resemblance to Bill Cowher, Steelers fans "hate Steely." As one fan wrote on a website, "We the members of Steeler Nation are now embarrassed. Steely McBeam does not represent the toughness of our city or of our team."

The San Antonio Missions' Henry the Puffy Taco. The mascot of Seattle's Double-A affiliate offends Raymond's sensibilities because "he wanted me to run over him with my four-wheeler. He was a little crazy."

The Villanova University Wildcat. Raymond's reason for disliking him is very simple: "My father is former University of Delaware football coach Tubby Raymond, and we both hated the Wildcat. Hey, I can't be balanced all the time."

> "Wives of ballplayers, when they teach their children their prayers, should instruct them to say: 'God bless Mommy, God bless Daddy and God bless Babe Ruth, who has upped Daddy's paycheck by 15 to 40 percent."
> —Hall of Famer and Ruth teammate Waite Hoyt

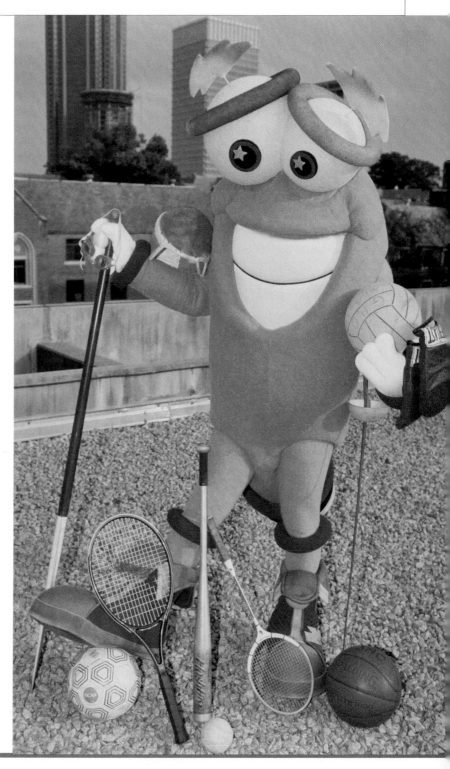

"We have a great bunch of outside shooters. Unfortunately, all our games are played indoors."
—New Mexico State basketball coach Weldon Drew

1996 Olympics mascot Izzy.

UP A TREE

If you're looking for a college mascot that embodies creativity, spirit, and the fine line between irreverence and anarchy, look no farther than Palo Alto, California. There, you will find the Stanford Tree, born in 1976 after a contest to determine who or what would replace the politically incorrect Prince Lightfoot. (Losing out were a manhole and a french fry.) The first sapling happened to be the band manager's girlfriend. Tree Week arrived in 1987, a highly rigorous period that has involved leeches, staged fights, bribery, and BB guns.

Patrick "Patchez" Fortune was the man behind the leaves in 2008, and as you can see by his personal, almost comprehensible game-day diary, it's not easy being green:

10:00 A.M. Rise and shine! I shake off the morning dew and stretch my branches. Something smells funky. Oh wait, it's just my magical vest (the only remaining part of the original Tree costume). I limber up by performing my extensive stretch routine—the grueling dance workout this afternoon doesn't take well to wooden trunks.

12 NOON. Down three raw eggs. Suppress a gag. I think I'll try wheatgrass shots next week. I need to watch my weight.

12:05 P.M. Check out my sylvan appearance in the mirror. Chicks dig leaves. I align my floppy Cyclops eye in the center, fix my sparse leaves. (No, I'm not balding, just a work in progress.) I polish my pearly whites with some Pine-Sol.

12:15 P.M. Unlock my Treecycle from the bike rack. Ride to the tailgate via my eco-friendly mode of transportation. Make sure to avoid the Claw fountain, which nearly claimed the life of one of my predecessors.

12:30 P.M. Feed me! I wander around the tailgate scrounging for food. Sometimes photosynthesis just doesn't cut it.

1:30 P.M. Find my bandmates, the Leland Stanford Junior University Marching Band (LSJUMB for short). I admire the Dollies (our esteemed white-gloved dancers) and give each one a little Tree bump.

1:45 P.M. Breathalyzer conducted by the Palo Alto Police Department. Too bad I can't use a urine sample for this. I just have to Tree up. The last time we had a Tree felled by inebriation, things got ugly.

> "I'm tired of hearing about money, money, money, money, money. I just want to play the game, drink Pepsi, wear Reebok."
> —Shaquille O'Neal

2:00 P.M. Game time! Before I hit the field for my opening gambol, I take a moment to meditate. *I am the one.*

2:00 P.M.–5:00 P.M. Follow Tree motto: *Maintain*. We beat San Jose State 28–10.

5:00 P.M. I make like a Tree and leaf. Actually, I'm escorted out by the Tree Protective Services, who have to strong-arm their way through belligerent fans and adoring Stanfordites.

5:30 P.M. Time to make an appearance at various postgame celebrations around the Farm.

2:30 A.M. Lights out. Sleep tight, and don't let the termites bite.

GREENER GRASS

I f you've ever marveled at a beautiful manicured playing field, or even if you just want grass that's always greener, meet George Toma, the oft-proclaimed God of Sod. Toma, author of *Nitty Gritty Dirt Man*, is now officially retired as the groundskeeper for both the Kansas City Chiefs and the Kansas City Royals. Having helped prepare the field for every Super Bowl ever played, he offers these guidelines for starting a field from scratch:

1. Select your space. Whatever area you choose for a field, whether it's a lot or a backyard, be sure it's a safe place for children.

2. Clear away any rocks, stumps, roots, broken glass, bottles, and debris. Look over the lot for depressions. Decide whether the lot is bare dirt or if it's loaded with weeds. If there's some grass down that you want to save, you can put down a fertilizer with a herbicide, called a weed and feed. If it's all weeds, sometimes it's best to just cover the whole thing with weed killer, such as Roundup. This is a job for adults, not kids.

3. Have an adult rent a lawn aerator from a hardware store like Home Depot. An Aerifier punches holes in the ground and loosens up the soil that is compacted. It's better to do this with a machine rather than by hand because it would just take too much time and effort. If your lot is in bad shape, you might have to go over it multiple times.

4. Now it's testing time. Take a spoonful of soil from the holes the aerator made—down at least 2 inches—from various areas of your lot. Mix them together before sending it off to the local agricultural cooperative in your county. Universities also often have a testing laboratory. For a minimal fee, they test the soil to see if you need lime or other treatments to regulate the pH. The lab can tell you what soil type you have, what grass species and fertilizer to use. They'll tell you what mineral elements are missing, if you need nitrogen, potash, or phosphorus.

5. You'll need to use different seeds depending on where you live. If you live in the transition zone—that's the upper half of the country, from about St. Louis up—you'll need to use cool-season grasses, like fescues, perennial ryegrass,

and Kentucky bluegrass. If you live in the lower portion of the country, Bermuda grass works well.

6. Next, prepare the seedbed. You'll need to rent a Verticut machine, which is used to cut grooves into the ground that the seeds will drop into. Again, take it through your land more than once. It's best to take it through two ways, creating a crosshatch.

7. After you decide on what type of seed you're going to use, measure out your field and use the amount of seed at the recommended rate for square footage. It will be on the bag of seed. You'll measure out the seed and spread it out. You can do this by hand or by using a seed spreader. Fertilizer goes down next. You only need a small amount. Again, read the directions so you use the proper amount.

8. Water your land. It should be moist but not saturated. That might mean watering one to three times a day, keeping the seed moist so it will germinate. In the northern part of the country, September, October, November is Mother Nature's time to seed a field. In the South, it would be in the spring.

9. When your lawn has grown, mow it no lower than an inch and a half. With the Bermuda grass, you can mow it down to an inch.

Legendary grounds keeper George Toma tends the turf during the Chicago Bears' 20–12 victory over the Philadelphia Eagles in the 1988 NFC divisional playoff game at Soldier Field.

Now, if you want to experiment a little and see what the grass will look like, Toma says you can try pregermination. Here's something even kids can do:

1. Take an old nylon stocking, cut the heel off, and tie a knot at one end.

2. Put a half pound of seed in the stocking.

3. Place the stocking with the seeds in a bucket of water—we do this for the Super Bowl, where we have 10 to 20 55-gallon barrels.

4. If you put the seed in the water at 8 A.M., at 5 or 6 P.M. replace the water. (You put it in the stocking so the seeds don't float out when you dump the old water out.) This gets the jump on the germination.

5. Do this for three days. By then, the seeds should be popping.

THE CRADLE THE ESSENCE OF LACROSSE

The cradle is the essential action of lacrosse. Without a good one, you can't run down the field with the ball without losing it. Here are a few tips on proper cradling:

1. Put your dominant hand right under the throat of the head of the stick. This will be the hand you are using to control the stick. Place your bottom hand loosely at the very bottom of the stick over the butt end. Remember, you will be controlling the stick entirely with your top hand; the bottom hand is only for stability.

2. Roll your top wrist to its full extension while using your bottom hand loosely to stabilize the stick, making a loose C shape with the thumb and fingers of your bottom hand. When cradling, you should feel the weight of the ball in the stick.

3. Cradle back and forth about a foot in front of your face. Keep your stick at a 45- to 60-degree angle to the ground and directly in front of your face.

4. Practice picking up ground balls. To do this, throw a few balls on the ground, get your elbows locked, and scoop the ball up. Be sure to bend your knees and get your stick as parallel to the ground as you can in order to ensure the retrieval of the ball. Don't stop when the ball is in your stick, but go through it and drop your bottom hand down in order to keep the ball in your stick.

If lacrosse itself had a cradle, it would be Maryland. It's 19th in population of the 50 states and 42nd in area, but it's generally acknowledged as the sport's most fertile ground. "The beauty of it is that it was kind of accidental," says Joe Finn, the archivist for US Lacrosse. "It just happened."

Back in 1878, members of the Baltimore Athletic Club attended a lacrosse match in Newport, Rhode Island. They were so enthralled by the sport, then mostly played in Canada, that they brought equipment home with them and started playing games. By 1882, the BAC had moved its practice facility close to Johns Hopkins University, and students at the school quickly fell in love with the sport. In 1908, the U.S. Naval Academy, in Annapolis, took up lacrosse, and two years later the University of Maryland joined in the fun.

Johns Hopkins has won nine Division I national championships, and Maryland two. Salisbury University, also in Maryland, has won eight Division III titles. Two more Maryland colleges, Loyola and Towson, have fielded strong teams. The National Lacrosse Hall of Fame is in Baltimore. (Its members outnumber those of the Baseball Hall of Fame, 343–286.)

So how come the state sport of Maryland is jousting?

THE BIGGER THEY COME . . .
A SPORTS PROMOTION GONE WRONG

L acrosse in Maryland provides the backdrop for one of history's most ill-fated sports promotions. Back in the 1970s, the National Lacrosse League was trying to get people interested in box (indoor) lacrosse, and Andy Dolich was the VP of business operations for the Maryland Arrows. "Our marketing slogan was 'You gotta be mean to play box lacrosse,' and our mascot was a cartoon character called Crunch Crosscheck," says Dolich, who went on to serve as an executive with the Oakland A's, the Memphis Grizzlies, and the San Francisco 49ers. "That should give you some idea of our level of sophistication."

Anyway, I hatched a scheme that we were going to call Guaranteed Shutout Night. We would give free tickets to the next home game if our opponents scored a goal.

Even though the goal is 4 feet high and 4.9 feet wide, a shutout is no easy feat. Teams usually score in double figures. But I had this idea:

If I could find a large human being, put him in uniform with the goalie pads, and jam him in the goal, all he had to do would be to stand there and—voilà—we would shut out the other team. So I found an over-the-hill wrestler named Man Mountain Mike, who was 6-foot-5 and 600 pounds. We suited him up and brought him to practice to see how this would work before we went public.

After the first few practice shots bounced off the Mountain, the Arrows decided to turn up the heat.

Our star player, Paul Suggate, was one of the NLL's leading scorers and had a laser shot, which he could pinpoint with surgical precision. Suggate comes in and launches a missile right at the family jewels, and Mountain goes down in a landslide. It seems he didn't put on a cup. As he was carted off on a stretcher, my dreams of Guaranteed Shutout Night went out with him.

WRESTLING

25¢

NWA

SARASOTA
SATURDAY, OCT. 21, 1972

COACH'S CORNER

by John Heath

Seventeen top heavyweights will compete in an over the top rope battle royal tonight. This is one of the most spectacular--and one of the most dangerous--events in professional wrestling.

One of the contestants in this event is Man Mountain Mike, the acknowledged king

---

17 MAN
OVER-THE-TOP-ROPE
Battle Royal
featuring Man Mountain Mike

Florida Heavyweight
Title Match

PAUL JONES
champion

—vs.—

DALE LEWIS

---

6 Man Tag Team Match

**JACK BRISCO - MIKE GRAHAM
& LOUIE TILLET**

—vs.—

**BOBBY SHANE - BUDDY COLT
& MIKE WEBSTER**

TIM WOODS vs. **MIKE PAIDOUSIS**

BOB ORTON SR. & BOB ORTON JR.

—— vs. ——

SPUTNIK MONROE & NORVEL AUSTIN

PHIL ROBLEY vs. **BOB GRIFFIN**

MAN MOUNTAIN MIKE

of battle royal competition. Mike tips the scales at over 600 pounds, so naturally it is rather difficult for opponents to toss this big fellow over the top rope.

Paul Jones will defend the Florida heavyweight title against the challenge of Dale Lewis. Dale, who has one of the most impressive amateur records in professional wrestling, once held the Florida title. At 265 pounds, Lewis is one of the most respected athletes in wrestling.

Jack Brisco, Mike Graham and Louie Tillet will team up to face Bobby Shane,

Buddy Colt and Mike Webster in a six man tag team event.

Mike Graham's success in the pro ranks is a matter of considerable pride for me, since I coached him when he was just a little fellow. Another of my pupils, Bob Orton, Jr., has just turned pro and will be teamed up with his father to wrestle Florida tag team champs Sputnik Monroe and Norvel Austin.

Tim Woods will go against the rugged veteran, Mike Paidousis. Opening action has Phil Robley against Bob Griffin.

Man Mountain Mike fills the cover of Wrestling *magazine, 1972.*

MIGHTIEST FIGHT (NONBOXING)
THE DAY SANTA CLAUS DROPPED HIS GLOVES

Christmas Eve 2005. Peace on earth, goodwill toward men. Except at the Nassau Coliseum, where a New York Islanders promotion offering free tickets to anyone dressed as Santa Claus went awry. Some 500 Santas showed up for the game against the Philadelphia Flyers, more than twice the number expected, and all of them were invited to walk across the ice between the first and second periods.

The trouble started when a few of the Santas ripped off their red jackets to reveal—gasp!—New York Rangers jerseys. To put it mildly, the fans of the Islanders and the fans of the Rangers are like the Jets and the Sharks. The dis was too much for the Islander Santas, who swarmed the Ranger Santas, and a brawl ensued. One junior Kringle was seen trying to pull a Pavel Bure Rangers sweater over the head of one of the subversives. It took a full nine minutes for order to be restored, as the public-address announcer kept saying, "All Santas will be escorted from the building." Fortunately, nobody was hurt.

The Islanders won the game, 4–2, on two goals by Arron Asham. Told about the fight, Asham said, "Really? That's awesome. I hope they have that on tape." You can find it on YouTube, under "Santafight."

> **The only doubleheader in NHL history was held on March 3, 1968, at Madison Square Garden (Flyers-Seals, Rangers-Blackhawks) because the roof at Philadelphia's Spectrum had blown off in a snowstorm.**

"**All hockey players are bilingual. They know English and profanity.**"
—Gordie Howe

FORE SCORE THE BEST PRESIDENTIAL GOLFER MIGHT SURPRISE YOU

Among all American presidents, who was the best golfer? Before you answer, here's a warning: It's a trick question.

The answer isn't Dwight David Eisenhower (number 34). Even though Ike played more golf than any of his peers, he never scored better than the low 90s. It isn't Gerald Ford (number 38), who was a better athlete than he was a hacker. "I know I'm getting better," he once said, "because I'm hitting fewer spectators." Nor was it Bill Clinton (number 42), whose skills were overshadowed by his billigan ethics.

Ulysses Grant (number 18) was the first president to play golf and thus the first to discover the 19th hole. At 330 pounds, William H. Taft (number 27) was the biggest president to play golf, and though he helped popularize the game, critics accused him of spending too much time on the links. George W. Bush (number 43) was once a 15 handicap, but he dropped the game shortly after he was interviewed on the first tee at Congressional Country Club in Bethesda, Maryland. After telling the interviewer, "I call upon all nations to do everything they can to stop these terrorist killings," Bush blurted out, "Now watch this drive!"

> **Gene Littler won the 1961 U.S. Open with a putter he had discovered at a miniature golf course.**

We've kept you in suspense long enough. The best golfer among our chief executives was none other than Franklin Delano Roosevelt (number 32). FDR fell in love with golf as a teenager, and by the time he left Harvard to attend Columbia Law School, he was scoring consistently in the low 80s. According to Don Van Natta Jr., in his book *First Off the Tee,* Roosevelt made sure to squeeze in a couple of rounds at St. Andrews during his honeymoon in Europe with Eleanor in 1905. After Woodrow Wilson (number 28), who once took 15 putts to finish a hole, appointed him assistant secretary of the navy in 1913, Roosevelt established himself as one of the best golfers in D.C.

But in 1921, he was stricken with polio, and according to Eleanor he never so much as uttered the word "golf" again. Still, the game never left his mind. On

December 8, 1941, a White House photographer captured FDR signing
the declaration of war against Japan as senators and congressmen looked on.
There, on his desk, was a cigarette lighter in the shape of a golf ball.

*FDR tees off at
Campobello, 1904.*

HARDWARE STORIES
THE TALES BEHIND SOME FAMOUS TROPHIES

Besides the fact that they are three of sports' most coveted trophies, what do the Stanley Cup, the World Cup, and the Claret Jug have in common? Well, for one thing, each has to be returned before a new champion has won it. And for another, they have rich histories befitting their 328 combined years of presentation.

The Claret Jug

Officially known as the Golf Champion Trophy, a replica of the original 1873 silver jug is presented to the winner of the British Open, which is officially known as The Open Championship. The original Open trophy was the Challenge Belt, leather with a silver buckle, but Tom Morris Jr. retired it after winning the Open three straight times (1868–70). After a year's hiatus, the Open resumed in 1872, but the cup wasn't commissioned until two days before the tournament, which Morris won again, over seven other players. So the first golfer to receive the jug, valued at £30 and made by Mackay Cunningham and Company of Edinburgh, was the 1873 winner, Tom Kidd. Morris, as the first winner, was the first to have his name engraved on the trophy.

Tiger Woods kisses the Claret Jug after winning the 135th Open Championship at Royal Liverpool Golf Club in Hoylake, England, on July 23, 2006.

> "Reverse every natural instinct and do the opposite of what you are inclined to do, and you will probably come very close to having a perfect golf swing."
>
> —Ben Hogan

After Bobby Jones won the 1927 Open, the Royal and Ancient Golf Club decided that henceforth it would retain the cup while the winner would keep a replica for a year. The original is on display in the R&A Clubhouse, along with the Challenge Belt. Replicas are also on display at the British Golf Museum in St. Andrews and in two traveling exhibitions. Open winners often commission their own replica to keep.

When Mark Calcavecchia won the Open in 1989, he said, "How's my name going to fit on that thing?" As the most recent winner, Pádraig Harrington, held the jug, his four-year-old son, Paddy, asked, "Dad, can we put ladybirds in it?"

> "One minute you're bleeding. The next minute you're hemorrhaging. The next minute you're painting the *Mona Lisa*."
> —former PGA Tour pro Mac O'Grady

The World Cup

There have actually been two trophies presented to the winner since the first World Cup tournament in 1930—make that three, but we'll get to that.

The first was the Jules Rimet Trophy, originally named Victory and later renamed for the FIFA president who initiated the tournament. Made of gold-plated sterling silver and lapis lazuli, it depicted Nike, the Greek goddess of victory. After Italy won the World Cup in 1938, Italian FIFA official Ottorino Barassi secretly transported Victory from a bank in Rome and hid it in a shoe box under his bed to prevent the Nazis from absconding with it. (The trophy was returned when the war ended.)

Four months before the 1966 World Cup, in England, the trophy was stolen from an exhibition at Central Hall Westminster. It was found just seven days later, wrapped in a newspaper at the base of a garden hedge in Norwood, in South London, by a black-and-white mongrel named Pickles. When England won the Cup, Pickles was invited to the celebration banquet, where he licked the plates clean.

Pickles, the hero of the 1966 World Cup.

When Brazil won the tournament for the third time, in 1970, it was allowed to keep Victory, according to Rimet's stipulation that the first three-time winner should retain it. The cup was stolen again in 1983, however, from the Brazilian Football Confederation in Rio de Janeiro, and never recovered. (Alas, Pickles could not be sent to search for it—he had died in 1973 when he choked on his leash while chasing a cat.) Brazil is now in possession of a replica.

The second World Cup (or the third, if you count the Brazilian replica of Victory) is called simply the FIFA World Cup, and it depicts two human figures holding up the globe. Made of solid gold with a malachite base, it is now in the possession of the Italian Soccer Federation. Fabio Cannavaro, Italy's captain, was photographed a few days after the 2006 World Cup holding a piece of green malachite that had broken off the base. The shard has since been glued back into place.

The Stanley Cup

The holy grail of hockey dates back to 1892, when Lord Stanley, Canada's governor general, purchased a silver bowl for 10 guineas ($48.67), to be presented each year to Canada's top hockey team, which in 1893 was the Montreal Amateur Athletic Association's hockey club. In 1907, the bowl went to the team from the small town of Kenora, Ontario (population 4,000). The Cup went pro in 1915, and by 1926 it belonged to the National Hockey League.

By then, a band had been added to the base to accommodate the engraving of the names of the winners. In 1958, the present-day Cup took shape: a five-band barrel containing enough space for the names of 65 teams. Whenever the bottom band is maxed out, the top band is sent to the Hockey Hall of Fame, in Toronto, and a blank is added to maintain the Cup's signature look.

A great deal of lore comes with the trophy. In 1907, before losing to Kenora, the Montreal Wanderers left it behind after a team picture, and the photographer's mother turned it into a flowerpot. Several members of the Montreal Canadiens left it in a roadside

snowbank after repairing a flat tire; when they returned, mortified, it was still there. Bryan Trottier of the New York Islanders once unscrewed the bowl and used it as a food dish for his dog. More typically, players sip champagne from it, and the Cup has been known to make appearances in late-night establishments.

For those and other reasons, the Cup now has a full-time bodyguard. One was in Sweden in the summer of 2008, when Tomas Holmström of the Detroit Red Wings had his day with the Cup. He used it to baptize his seven-week-old niece, Alva Felicia.

Anaheim Ducks goaltender Jean-Sébastien Giguère (not pictured) put his infant son, Maxime, in the Stanley Cup after defeating the Ottawa Senators in Game 5 of the 2007 Stanley Cup finals.

A BUMP UP
YOU MAY NEVER BE A MOGUL, BUT YOU CAN SKI ONE

It's one thing to be able to cruise down a nicely groomed ski slope looking good, but as any expert skier knows, the real fun to be had on a mountain is in the bumps. At first, trying to navigate uneven terrain with 4- to 5-foot planks on your feet may seem daunting, but Aspen Highlands Ski School manager Andy Docken says that turning on moguls—provided you can make short turns on groomed surfaces—is actually easier. Here are his tips for skiing the bumps:

Don't Ski Them like a Pro. There are three ways to tackle moguls, Docken says. The easiest way is to ski up the back of the bump and make your turn on top, when the tips and tails of your skis are not touching the snow. It's a good way to get comfortable, but it's not very fast or very fun. What the pros do is the opposite: They make their turns in the troughs between bumps, aka the zipper line. (Imagine where blue paint would end up if you dumped a can of it at the top of a mogul field—that's the zipper line.) Unless your name is Tomba, you don't want to do that either. But you want to do something close to it. "Intermediate skiers first getting into moguls should ski a rounder line," Docken says, meaning that they should turn on the side of the bump, just above the zipper line. "Because you're turning on the bank," he explains, "you don't have to focus on putting your ski on its edge so much. It's deflection, so it's actually easier." Skiing a rounder line also keeps your speed in check.

Imagine a Ceiling. "When skiing moguls, always keep your head at the same level," Docken says. "Make believe there is a ceiling that you don't want to put your head through." Your head should just be touching this ceiling when you are standing tall at the lowest point between moguls. As you go up the bump, flex your knees to make your legs shorter; as you go down the bump, straighten your knees to extend your legs. (This move is often referred to as absorbing the bump.) "People tend to get real compact in moguls," Docken warns. "Make sure your legs get long as you go down the backside." Your skis should maintain contact with the snow at all times—there should be no hopping from turn to turn.

Use Your Turn Signals. You have ski poles for a reason. You don't necessarily "plant" them, but you should touch them to the ground before turning. "Touch the right pole before making a right turn and the left pole before making a left turn," Docken says. The pole plant should come at the point when you switch your weight from one ski to the other, and the pole should touch the uphill-facing side of the bump you are about to turn on. As always when skiing, but even more important in moguls, keep your weight over your feet, and keep your upper body quiet and facing downhill at all times; let your lower body do all the turning. Last, focus your eyes on your line three to four turns ahead.

One more thing. Since many mogul runs are under chairlifts, you'll be performing in front of a live audience. If at first that seems like a negative, don't worry. Soon enough, other skiers will be wishing they were you.

THE VOICE OF GOD THE NFL'S GREATEST STORYTELLER, JOHN FACENDA

His full name was John Thomas Ralph Augustine James Facenda, but his nickname was even more impressive: the Voice of God. Citizens of Philadelphia knew him, and his mellifluent tones, well because he anchored television news in that city for two decades. Indeed, his signature sign-off—"Have a nice night tonight and a good day tomorrow. Good night, all"—is featured in the 1957 movie *The Burglar*, starring Jayne Mansfield and Dan Duryea.

But it was as the original narrator of NFL Films that Facenda became a household voice: deep and dramatic, staccato and sincere. Facenda got the NFL gig quite by accident. One night in 1965, he and another newscaster, Jack Whitaker, were in Philadelphia's RDA Club, which happened to be showing slow-motion game sequences filmed by Ed Sabol, the founder of NFL Films. Recalled Facenda, "I started to rhapsodize about how beautiful it was. Ed Sabol . . . came up to me and asked, 'If I give you a script, could you repeat what you just did?' I said I would try."

Thus began an association that would last until Facenda's death, in 1984, at the age of 71. In life, Facenda was known for his generosity and grace. But he will also always be known for "The Autumn Wind," a tribute to the 1974 Oakland Raiders written by Steve Sabol:

> The autumn wind is a pirate
> Blustering in from sea;
> With a rollicking song he sweeps along,
> Swaggering boisterously.
> His face is weatherbeaten,
> He wears a hooded sash,
> With a silver hat about his head
> And a bristling black mustache.
> He growls as he storms the country,
> A villain big and bold,
> And the trees all shake and quiver and quake
> As he robs them of their gold.
> The autumn wind is a Raider,
> Pillaging just for fun.
> He'll knock you 'round and upside down
> And laugh when he's conquered and won.

That stentorian music still reverberates. John Facenda Jr. recently sued NFL Films over the unauthorized use of his father's voice.

THE LUCKIEST SPEECH

The most famous speech in sports was almost never given. Lou Gehrig, afflicted with amyotrophic lateral sclerosis, had his number 4 retired by the Yankees in between the games of the July 4, 1939, doubleheader, and he was so overcome with emotion that he started to walk off the field without saying a word. The stadium crew had even begun to remove the pile of gifts he had received. But many in the crowd of 55,000 chanted "Lou, Lou," beseeching the ordinarily shy slugger to speak. So Gehrig turned around and went back to the microphones. The crowd fell silent, and this is what he said:

Fans, for the past two weeks you have been reading about the bad break. Yet today I consider myself the luckiest man on the face of the earth. I have been in ballparks for 17 years and have never received anything but kindness and encouragement from you fans.

Look at these grand men. Which of you wouldn't consider it the highlight of his career just to associate with them for even one day? Sure, I'm lucky. Who wouldn't have considered it an honor to have known Jacob Ruppert? Also, the builder of baseball's greatest empire, Ed Barrow? To have spent six years with that wonderful little fellow Miller Huggins? Then to have spent the next nine years with that outstanding leader, that smart student of psychology, the best manager in baseball today, Joe McCarthy? Sure, I'm lucky.

When the New York Giants, a team you would give your right arm to beat, and vice versa, sends you a gift, that's something. When everybody down to the groundskeepers and those boys in white coats remember you with trophies, that's something. When you have a wonderful mother-in-law who takes sides with you in squabbles against her own daughter, that's something. When you have a father and mother who work all their lives so you can have an education and build your body, it's a blessing. When you have a wife who has been a tower of strength and shown more courage than you dreamed existed, that's the finest I know.

So I close in saying that I might have been given a bad break, but I have an awful lot to live for.

Lou Gehrig, July 4, 1939.

Acknowledgments

We hope this book reflects the joy of being part of a team because it was just that: a glorious experience shared by a lot of talented individuals. I'd first like to thank the mighty contributors who suggested and submitted the items for this book: Adena Andrews, Gary Belsky, Elena Bergeron, Lindsay Berra, Jeff Bradley, Dale Brauner, David Carlyon, Anna K. Clemmons, Larue Cook, Garland Cooper, Charles Curtis, Michelle Daum, Lindsey Dolich, Bethany Donaphin, David Duberstein, Tom Farrey, Neil Fine, Matt Giles, the late great Joey Goldstein, Steve Hirdt, Michael Hudson, Jerushah Ismail, Roger Jackson, Aaron Kennedi, Tom Lakin, Henry Lee, Jonathan Lesser, Jamie Lowe, Jeffrey Lyons, Ndidi Massay, John Mastroberardino, Ryan McGee, Ed McGregor, Doug McIntyre, Dave McKee, Doug Mittler, Daniel Okrent, Will Petersen, Dave Raymond, Harold Richman, Howie Schwab, Greg Segal, Ed Shanahan, Mickey Steiner, Wendy Taylor, Craig Thompson, Rob Tringali, Bill Vourvoulias, Glen Waggoner, Craig Winston, Gene Wojciechowski, Michael Woods, and Bo Wulf. Deep appreciation to the folks who lent moral, logistical, and creative support to *The Mighty Book:* Sandy DeShong, Gary Hoenig, Chris Raymond, Richard Rosen, Ellie Seifert, and Perry van der Meer at ESPN Books; Christine Cabello, Ben Dreyer, Lisa Feuer, Kim Hovey, Carole Lowenstein, Mark Maguire, Libby McGuire, Steve Messina, Cindy Murray, Daniel Pelavin, Alex Rudd, Scott Shannon, David Stevenson, Paul Taunton, Mark Tavani, and Lisa Turner at Ballantine. Thanks, too, to Gregory Proch and Christian Rogers, our go-to illustrators, and Joe Rodriguez, our go-to photographer. A special shout-out to John Glenn, who juggled text, illustration, and production with grace and dexterity. Last but certainly not least, we all owe a debt of gratitude to Beth Tondreau, who made the whole enterprise come alive with a design that speaks to the eternity, variety, and beauty of sports.

Photography and Illustration Credits

On pages with more than one image, credits are given clockwise from top left.

Page i: Cornell rowers, illustration by John E. Sheridan, c. 1902 (Library of Congress) • page ii: sports cards produced by various American tobacco companies, c. 1872–1918 (Advertising Ephemera Collection, Emergence of Advertising On-Line Project, John W. Hartman Center for Sales, Advertising & Marketing History, Duke University Rare Book, Manuscript, and Special Collections Library) • page iv: football player, illustration by Edward Penfield, c. 1913 (Library of Congress) • page ix: Native American youths in Florida, engraving by Theodor de Bry, c. 1591 (Library of Congress) • pages x and xii: sports memorabilia (courtesy Steve Wulf/photographs by Joe Rodriguez) • pages xiv–1: Caledonian games, lithograph by J. L. Giles, c. 1868 (Library of Congress) • page 3: John Wooden, Lew Alcindor, and UCLA freshmen, 1965 (UCLA Charles E. Young Research Library Department of Special Collections, *Los Angeles Times* Photographic Archives, copyright © Regents of the University of California, UCLA Library) • pages 4–5: pass pattern illustrations by Christian Rogers • page 5: football player, illustration by Hibberd V. B. Kline, c. 1910 (Library of Congress) • page 7: Jeff Gordon's pit crew, 2008 (Getty Images for NASCAR) • page 8: Lou Gehrig, 1925 (Library of Congress) • page 10: illustrations by Gregory Proch • page 11: baseball card, c. 1911 (Library of Congress) • page 12: Henry Chadwick, c. 1890 (MLB Photos via Getty Images) • page 13: *Beadle's Dime Base-ball Player*, 1873 (courtesy Dennis C. Purdy) • pages 14–15: Phil Mickelson, 2007 (PGA/Getty Images) • page 16: reporters at Polo Grounds, 1913 (Library of Congress) • page 18: Sharpie pen (photograph by Joe Rodriguez) • page 19: David Wright, 2007 (Getty Images) • page 20: illustrations by Gregory Proch • page 21: *Field of Dreams* movie poster (The Kobal Collection) • page 22: Wade Boggs and Marty Barrett, 1981 (photograph by Ralph Smith/courtesy Pawtucket Red Sox) • page 23: baseball line score illustration (courtesy Pawtucket Red Sox); illustration from tobacco package label showing baseball players, c. 1869 (Library of Congress) • page 25: Amos Alonzo Stagg, 1928 (Getty Images) • page 26: Wayne Gretzky, 1998 (Getty Images) • page 27: Georgeann Wells (West Virginia University) • page 28: Michael Phelps Wheaties box (Getty Images) • page 29: Joe Hauser baseball card, 1961, and Babe Ruth Wheaties advertisement, 1956 (courtesy Dennis C. Purdy) • page 30: illustration by Gregory Proch • page 31: Everett Case, 1959 (Time & Life Pictures/Getty Images) • page 32: Jim Valvano, 1993 (ESPN) • page 33: illustration from Wilson basketball advertisement, 1920 • page 34: Ted Williams, 1957 (Time & Life Pictures/Getty Images) • page 35: Lance Alworth, 1970 (Getty Images) • pages 36–37: illustrations by Gregory Proch • page 38: Pete Sheehy plaque (Getty Images) • page 39: illustration by Gregory Proch • page 41: Muhammad Ali and Joe Frazier, 1971 (Getty Images) • page 42: illustration by Gregory Proch • page 43: Stump the Schwab logo (ESPN) • page 44: Magic Johnson, 1987 (Getty Images) • page 45: Jim Brown, 1965, and Sandy Koufax, 1965 (Getty Images) • page 49: WPA Field Day poster, 1939 (Library of Congress) • page 50: Brian Roberts, 2008 (Getty Images) • page 51: George Sherrill, 2008 (Getty Images) • page 53: Gerald Ford, 1934 (NFL/Getty Images) • pages 54–55: Rucker Park, 2008 (Getty Images) • page 56: cover of *Harper's*, color lithograph by Edward Penfield, April 1898 (Library of Congress); tug-of-war event, 1920 Olympic Games (Getty Images) • page 57: Bobby Jones, 1927 (Getty Images) • pages 58–59: broadcast footage, 2005 (courtesy Brian Collins and the Department of Telecommunications, Ball State University) • pages 60–62: illustrations by Gregory Proch • page 63: Cincinnati Red Stockings, print published by Tuchfarber, Walkley & Moellmann, Cincinnati, Ohio, c. 1869 (Library of Congress) • pages 64–67: Donovan McNabb's locker (photographs courtesy of Anna Clemmons) • page 68: Cy Young, c. 1910 (Getty Images) • page 69: Cy Young award (MLB Photos via Getty Images) • page 70: Water Cube (Christian Kober/Getty Images) • page 71: Melbourne Cricket Ground (Getty Images); Ski Dubai (Getty Images) • page 72: Estádio do Maracanã (*National Geographic*/Getty Images); Indianapolis Motor Speedway (Getty Images); Wembley Stadium (Getty Images) • page 73: Rift Valley Province, Kenya (AP Photo/Ben Curtis) • page 75: Sugar Ray Robinson, 1951 (Getty Images) • page 76: football at Wrigley Field (Diamond Images/Getty Images) • page 78: hockey glove (photograph by Joe Rodriguez); olfactory system illustration (courtesy Patrick J. Lynch) • page 79: Powder Point School poster, illustration by Bristow Adams, c. 1903 (Library of Congress) • page 81: still from *Over the Top*, 1987 (The Kobal Collection) • page 83: illustration by Gregory Proch • page 84: Francis Ouimet's clubs (United States Golf Association) • page 85: man swinging golf club, watercolor by Edward Penfield, 1915 (Library of Congress) • page 86: title page for *Casey at the Bat*, 1912 (Library of Congress) • page 87: King Kelly baseball card, 1888 (Library of Congress) • page 88: Dan Quisenberry, 1979 (MLB Photos via Getty Images) • pages 90–91: Union prisoners at Salisbury, N.C., lithograph by Sarony, Major & Knapp, 1863 (Library of Congress) • page 93: Bob Beamon, 1968 (Getty Images) • page 95: Elvis Presto, 1989, and James Brown, 1997 (Getty Images); U2, 2002 (WireImage/Getty Images) • page 96: Pete Sampras, 2002 (Getty Images) • page 98: NFL passing stats screen grab (ESPN.com) • page 99: football game, illustration by Edward Penfield, c. 1884–1925 (Library of Congress) • page 100: Aaron Rodgers, 2008 (Getty Images) • page 102: planting ivy at Wrigley Field, 1937 (© George Brace/Brace Photo) • page 103: Moises Alou, 2002 (AFP/Getty Images) • pages 104–105: Michigan Marching Band, 2006 (Getty Images) • pages 106–107: illustrations by Gregory Proch • page 111: USA defeats USSR at hockey, 1980 (Getty Images) • page 113: Victory Gallop and Real Quiet, 1998 (AFP/Getty Images) • page 115: Tiger Woods, 2004 (AFP/Getty Images) • page 117: Wilt Chamberlain, 1962 (AP Photo/Paul Vathis) • page 118: Wiffle bat and ball (iStockphoto) • page 119: Lance Armstrong, 2000 (Getty Images) • page 121: Bobby Knight, 1985 (AP Photo) • page 122: Gertrude Ederle, 1926 (Getty Images) • page 125: Jean-Philippe Darche, 2007 (Getty Images) • pages 126–127: Strat-O-Matic cards (courtesy Strat-O-Matic Game Co.) • pages 128–129: *About Three Bricks Shy of a Load* (courtesy the University of Pittsburgh Press); *Ball Four* (courtesy Jim Bouton/Bulldog Publishing); *The Sweet Science* (courtesy Farrar, Straus and Giroux); *The Summer Game* (courtesy the University of Nebraska Press); *Picking Winners* (courtesy Houghton Mifflin Harcourt) • pages 130–131: *The National Game*, lithograph by Currier & Ives, c. 1860 (Library of Congress) • page 132: Oakland Raiders at Pro Football Hall of Fame, 2008 (Getty Images) • page 133: white football (Getty Images) • page 135: Chris Moneymaker, 2006 (Getty Images) • page 136: Evander Holyfield and Mike Tyson, 1997 (AFP/Getty Images) • page 137: Scott Rolen, 2004 (Getty Images) • page 138: Joe Jurevicius, 2001 (© 2008 Robert Tringali/All Rights Reserved) • page 141: Doug Flutie, 1984 (AP Photo/File) • page 143: Jacques Plante, 1959 (Time & Life Pictures/Getty Images); Chico Resch, 1970 (NHLI via Getty Images); Evgeni Nabokov, 2008 (Getty Images) • page 144: Bjorn Borg, 1980 (Getty Images) • page 147: Wang Chen, 2008 (AFP/Getty Images) • page 149: Chris Paul, 2008 (NBAE/Getty Images) • page 151: Erin Buescher, 2005 (NBAE/Getty Images) • page 152: Fred Merkle, 1918 (Library of Congress) • page 154: baseball card show, 1989 (Getty Images) • page 155: Sherry Magee baseball card, 1909–1911 (Library of Congress) • page 157: illustration by Gregory Proch • page 159: cast photo from *The Sandlot*, 1993 (The Kobal Collection) • page 161: Edith Green and John F. Kennedy, 1959 (Time & Life Pictures/Getty Images) • page 163: U.S. women's eight, 2008 (Getty Images) • page 165: illustration by Gregory Proch • page 166: Don Larsen and Yogi Berra, 1956 (Diamond Images/Getty Images) • page 168: George Gipp, 1920 (Collegiate Images/Getty Images) • page 171: Shecky Greene the man, 2001 (Getty Images); Shecky Greene the horse, 1973 (photo by Jim Raftery/Turfotos) • page 172: football practice (iStockphoto) • page 175: basketball game (*Boston Globe*/Dominic Chavez/Landov) • page 177: Lou Gehrig, Babe Ruth, and Jackie Mitchell, 1931 (Getty Images) • page 179: Phillie Phanatic (Getty Images) • page 181: Izzy (Getty Images) • page 182: Stanford Tree (David Gonzales/Stanford Athletics) • page 185: George Toma, 1988 (Getty Images) • page 186: Johns Hopkins lacrosse player, illustration by Bristow Adams, c. 1905 (Library of Congress) • page 189: *Wrestling* magazine cover, 1972 (courtesy Barry Rose/www.cwfarchives.com) • page 191: illustration by Gregory Proch • page 193: Franklin Delano Roosevelt, 1904 (courtesy Franklin Delano Roosevelt Library and Museum) • page 194: Tiger Woods, 2006 (WireImage/Getty Images) • page 196: Pickles, 1966 (Popperfoto/Getty Images) • page 197: Stanley Cup and baby, 2007 (Getty Images) • page 199: illustration by Gregory Proch • page 203: Lou Gehrig, 1939 (Getty Images) • pages 204–205: "Sure Catch" Sticky Fly Paper advertisement, c. 1853–1898 (Library of Congress) • page 206: "On, Wisconsin!" sheet music cover, 1910 (Library of Congress) • page 208: WPA Athletics poster, 1939 (Library of Congress) • page 210: *The Game Is Over*, photograph by S. Arakelyan, 1911 (Library of Congress).

About the Editor

STEVE WULF is the co-author (with Daniel Okrent) of the bestseller *Baseball Anecdotes* and (with Buck O'Neil and David Conrads) *I Was Right On Time*. Now a senior writer for *ESPN The Magazine*, Wulf has been on the staff of *Time* and *Sports Illustrated*. He has written for *Entertainment Weekly*, *Life*, *The Wall Street Journal*, and *The Economist*. A father of four, he lives in Westchester County, New York.

The Game Is Over: Harvard vs. Yale, 1911.